THE GIFT OF STOPPAGE TIME

MARK VINCENT LINCIR

Cover Design by Drew Dunlevy

www.Drewddesigns.com

Published by Leftback Publishing LLC

PMB 501 835 W. Warner Road, Suite 101

Gilbert, AZ 85233 USA

ISBN: 9780985127237

Live happy!

2012

Also by Mark Vincent Lincir

A SOCCER LIFE IN SHORTS

THE WORLD NEEDS MORE BELLY RUBS

For Taffy & Bryan

Love You

CHAPTER 1

Once his first touch let him down and the ball ran too far away from his foot, it was all over but the crying. I went flying in on him like I was shot out of a cannon; studs up and oblivious to the consequences. He recovered from his dreadful first touch and got to the ball before I did, which was his first mistake. Then he tried to cheekily flick the ball up and over my incoming tackle, which was his second mistake. He hopped as high as he could, the ball still stuck to his foot, but it wasn't high enough. As his legs rose, so did mine and when we finally did make contact with each other, it was him who wished that he never received that ball so poorly in the first place.

He went flying into the chest-high chain link fence that sat dangerously close to the sideline and I poked the ball cleanly away from him and out of bounds...I think. Either that or I got all of him and none of the ball. In any case, he was down and out and I was up and ready, for his teammates of course. And as if on cue, they came charging in from all directions.

My own loyal teammates were not too far behind...and the weekly crowd-pleasing, bench-clearing brawl was in full effect at Daniel's Field in San Pedro California, home to the dirtiest semi-professional soccer league in the United States. The Greater Los Angeles Soccer League was a league where the hackers were valued and worshipped as much as the magicians and the runners found themselves relegated to background duty in games that saw more flying elbows, head-butts and hip-high, two-footed tackles than fancy step-overs, heel passes and nutmegs.

The blows to the back of my head pissed me off the most, because those knots took days to go away and the accompanying headaches made sleeping a restless endeavor. I also had dozens of angry hands clamoring for my jersey, trying to pull me in close enough to them to punch, head-butt, bite and kick me, but I wasn't having any of it, having been in these types of situations far too many times to get sucker-punched, especially on what was an otherwise gloriously sunny winter afternoon. As the pile of humanity tugged back and forth at each other and swayed to an unheard beat, the old men who leaned against the fence every Sunday dropped their cigarettes, clenched their fists and readied themselves for the opportunity to join the fray.

The supposedly injured victim of my beautifully-timed, premeditated, bone-wrenching tackle found his way to the flashpoint of the scrum and into my face. We were at the fence and I was being pushed up against it as my hands remained tied-up grabbing at jerseys and swinging wildly at the madness surrounding me. The short, stocky object of my tackle popped me with a head-butt to the underside of my chin that failed to draw blood, but did hurt just the same. As he pulled away from my face I saw a large, creased, tanned fist smash into his nose and turn it into a bloodied mess of mangled cartilage. I then found myself on the receiving end of another solid blow to the ear that came from the same direction of the blow that put my opponent down for the count. I turned towards the fence to see Tomislav, dressed in his suit and looking dapper as ever, shaking his perpetually-clenched right hand in front of his face trying to muster some life into it while he cussed himself in his native tongue.

We made eye contact with each other as the fight took its usual course and started to break up as the players, coaches and team managers tired and the two hulking, off-duty cops hired by the league to help the referees control what soccer-ignorant people simply referred to as games, intervened. Tomislav saw the concern on my face, but extinguished it with a knowing wink and I was once again left owing a sixty-year-old man who went to church every Sunday and still looked like he could play...a favor.

CHAPTER 2

It had been a decade since anyone gave a crap what I did with my life. Ten years since people took time out of their day to see what I was doing with mine. Ten years since tough, blue-collar men unabashedly gave me kisses on the cheek, stuffed money into my pockets and bought me drinks for shutting down the best strikers in the league. Ten years since grown men thanked God that they got to play with me instead of having to play against me. Ten years since women (some even pretty good-looking) patiently waited for me outside the locker rooms, hoping for an invite to the post-game party. Ten years since I felt like what I was doing with my life was having an impact on someone else's. Ten years since I was happy being me.

The most frustrating part about throwing it all away was that I was only thirty years old and my life had already become a cliché. I was the guy who was supposed to make it but didn't. Now I was home again, trying to do the best I could with the mess I had made of my life. I had the talent, the potential, the drive (at least for a while) and the opportunities. Every critical decision that I faced, I screwed up. Chances came and chances went and my decisions were always the same...the wrong ones.

So now I was home again, being a cliché, if you can even be such a thing. But it could have been worse, I could've been homeless and jobless and I was neither. I had a job on the docks that paid pretty good money when I did get the work and had a roof over my head, courtesy of my dad who grew tired of being lonely, moved up onto the hill, hit the Internet dating scene and had rarely been heard from since. Nevertheless, my waking hours were still consumed with guilt, regret and anger. I couldn't live with the fact that I was a should-have-been. I would have been much more comfortable being viewed as a has-been because in all fairness to them, they actually did accomplish something. I was just another talented guy from town that was supposed to make it but didn't and it ate me up inside. It tainted every minute of every day of my life, and I was getting extremely tired of it.

CHAPTER 3

The ball was tattered and gross. It looked like somebody barfed on it and then dunked it in an old tub of grease. Unfortunately, it also smelled like someone barfed on it and dunked it in a tub of grease. But Cowboy Chris, the only cowboy in the City of Los Angeles, who had never been on a horse or even to a rodeo, merrily bounced it up and down off the dock as the fog rolled out and the sun rose over one of the largest ports in the world. To Cowboy Chris, the mammoth-sized container ships that slowly passed by us on their way out into the open ocean were miracles of engineering. To me, they were just another in a long line of subliminal messages aimed at showing me how small I really was in this vast universe.

Cowboy Chris waved at every passing ship like it was a long-lost relative that he wouldn't see again until the holidays. He also used our daily dockside breaks to practice his Texas two-step. His inherent lack of coordination, coupled with a severe limp that he had since childhood, made watching his moves all but unbearable. But he obviously didn't care what anybody thought, because he kept doing it and sadly, not getting any better at it. I resented him for his unabashed enthusiasm towards the ships and their crews and wondered how he could have so much energy stored inside that little, pudgy body of his at the ungodly hour of six in the morning.

The ball unexpectedly took a bad bounce off an uneven piece of wood and came towards me. I didn't hesitate to rear back and full-volley it out into the channel. Cowboy Chris' perpetual, half-cocked grin quickly disappeared from his stubble-ridden face and the mood of the whole morning shifted from him-being-happy, me-being miserable, to him-being-miserable, me-being-happy. I was extremely proud of myself, if only for a moment.

"Now whaddya reckon I do?"

"Get back to work," I countered firmly.

He ignored the suggestion and slowly lit his umpteenth cigarette of the shift with his dirty hands. He inhaled deeply, his mind shifting itself into overdrive with the apparent help of nicotine.

"Ya think those guys play lots of cards?" He was obsessed with wondering what the crews on the huge ships that left our port did on their way to another continent.

"Probably," I said.

"I bet they work out a lot. Ya think they have a gym on those ships?"

"I'm sure some of them do."

"How awesome would it be to go out on a ship for weeks at a time?"

"Try months."

"Really, months? I'd love that life pardner. Just livin' out on the open seas for months at a time."

"I think that the novelty would wear off pretty quickly."

"Why ya always downplayin' stuff on me pardner? Ya don't think it would be awesome to be out there on the open seas, just you and your thoughts?" I didn't want to burst Cowboy Chris' bubble by informing him that the guys on the ships did work when they were out at sea. Cowboy Chris got excited about everything and anything and operated on a much more optimistic level than I did. I liked him too much to burst his bubble on a morning that actually was quite nice.

7

"It's probably a pretty cool life," I said appeasing his fantasy for the moment. Cowboy Chris shook his head enthusiastically at my endorsement of a lifestyle neither one of us knew anything about. The reason that I didn't disagree with Cowboy Chris was that he was that type of guy who could get you anything you needed without much notice and seemed to know everybody in town. I hadn't taken advantage of his reputation as the go-to guy yet, but was well-aware of his reputation around town and especially on the docks and always figured that somehow, someway, his talent would come in handy one day.

So I played along with his unhealthy infatuation with lifestyles he knew nothing about like we were talking about the man landing on the moon or the upcoming wedding of a good friend. Besides, he was one of the few guys I had seen since I got back into town that actually remembered me and some of my athletic exploits from back in the day. He claimed that we played on the same youth soccer team together and even though I looked through all my old team pictures and he wasn't in any of them, I liked him anyway. He reminded me of myself before life smacked me in the face with the harsh reality of having to cope with an unearned death as a teenager which made me as cynical, paranoid and angry as they came.

Cowboy Chris took another stab at his Texas two-step before his lame left foot dug into the dock and almost sent him reeling, face first, into the peculiarly-colored water below.

"Ya know, I never thought I'd see the day that you'd be down here on the docks with all of us," he said after recovering his balance and taking a lung-busting hit of his cigarette.

"I figured you'd be playin' in Europe or somethin', just being big-time out there in the world and all. But it's cool that you're back," he added. "Are ya glad to be back?"

I thought about all the things that brought me back home. There was the failed move to a southwest suburb that was supposed to inspire my then-girlfriend and I to settle down and get real about adult life, but instead had me squandering some of the best years of my life amidst a sterile and incredibly uninspiring backdrop of tract homes and strip malls. She enjoyed daily happy hours with her male co-workers and I got into fights with carpenters every day while I tried to sell fireplaces in the desert to make ends meet while constantly considering suicide even though I was petrified of blood and didn't even know how to fire a gun.

She wanted the formula and I didn't. It didn't work because it was never supposed to, but I tried to force it anyway in hopes that it would encourage me to grow into a serious adult. I found out the hard way how overrated that was. The inevitable conclusion of our relationship was an ugly break up that resulted in me catching a twelve-hour bus ride home with nothing but a backpack full of dirty clothes.

"Yeah, I'm glad to be back. Whoever said that you can't come home again was just stubborn," I asserted as I tried to make myself feel better about not pursuing a professional soccer career that I had dreamed of since birth.

"I reckon ya might just be right," he said.

"But I thought you said you never left town?"

"I haven't," Cowboy Chris said. We both laughed at the irony, even though I'm not sure that he realized that what he had said was so ironic. "Something about being home feels good," I said.

"But I also wonder if I've given up in a way, on trying to do something special with my life." Cowboy Chris crinkled his brow, dropped his cigarette on the ground and smashed it violently with his work boot.

"Hold on there pardner! Ya work in one of the busiest ports in the world. Helpin' move all this stuff to where it's supposed to go, now that's havin' an impact," Cowboy Chris said emphatically as he gestured with his hands to all the massive ships, containers and cranes that surrounded us.

"Yeah, I guess. It just seems like the more time I have on my hands, the less I do with it," I said dejectedly.

"It's probably just a phase pardner," he said as he laid a comforting hand on my shoulder.

"That phase you're talking about has been my entire adult life," I said.

"All ya can do is hang in there, it'll get better soon."

He suddenly yanked his hand off of my shoulder and side-stepped away from the edge of the dock. I turned around and saw a huge forklift headed straight for me. I took a step back, but ran out of room as the forklift skidded to a halt just inches from my face. I tried to hold my balance, but couldn't and reluctantly ended up falling ten feet into the water below. The water was cold and felt like it was clinging to my skin. I looked up from the water below at Cowboy Chris, who was laughing uncontrollably, almost to the point of tears.

"Welcome home pardner," he said.

"I'll get you for this," I said as I mockingly shook a fist at him.

"No ya won't," Cowboy Chris said as he and the driver disappeared from my view. I treaded water for a few minutes while I wondered if anyone was going to help me out of the water.

It didn't take long for me to realize that I was on my own. Then something bumped into the back of my head. I knew it wasn't a shark, but thought that it might be a dead body or serpent of some sort. I turned in a panic to see what it was as I fought to tread the cold morning water. It was the tennis ball, only this time it was nice and clean. It still smelled bad, really bad. I stared at it as it bobbed in front of my face while it stared back at me. It had come back to where it came from, just like me. I smiled, grabbed it and climbed out of the water with it firmly tucked under my arm.

CHAPTER 4

I had gotten to the point where I enjoyed walking around town. I had begun to notice things that I had never noticed before, like how far apart everything was, and how much easier owning a car would have made my life. The good part of my constant, involuntary strolling was that it let me wind down from the night of work and allowed me to ease into another day. I was all about easing into things because sudden changes never sat well with me even though I was forced to deal with one when I was only seventeen years old that changed my life forever.

I was walking past the parking lot and onto the main street when Cowboy Chris pulled up in his big, four-wheel drive behemoth of a truck. He must have had a dozen guys piled in the back of it. Some nodded to me, some glared at me for whatever reason...it was too early for me to get pissed about it and some looked indifferently at me as they lit their smokes and dialed their cell phones.

"Breakfast and beers, ya reckon ya might want to join us?" he asked.

"No thanks, I've got to get some work done on the house today."

"Ya ever gonna put a roof on that thing pardner?"

"Someday...maybe today."

"Yeah, right," he said as peeled out of the parking lot.

I continued, soaking wet, tired and moody on my journey home past the fishing boats, canneries and sailboat slips to the dank, over-crowded donut shop that I always stopped at on my way home.

The place was loud as ever with European men all trying to talk over each other as they guzzled their tar colored coffee and talked about everything from local politics to national soccer teams.

I stepped to the counter as I always did, scared as hell of the hard-looking man behind the counter who never said a single word to me in all the months I had been going there to get my coffee with cream and sugar and raspberry-filled donut to go. But before he handed me my bagged donut, he paused and inspected my appearance. A huge smile suddenly overcame his face that revealed teeth that had been neglected for far too long.

"You try out for svim team...yes?" He asked. The place went completely silent as all the men in the donut shop seemed to be astonished at his actually speaking of words. I knew better than to ever pop-off to one of the old-school guys, so the thought of disrespecting him never even crossed my mind. Unfortunately, I knew what he was getting at.

"Something like that," I said.

The whole shop erupted in laughter as the old man behind the counter was almost brought to tears by the impact of his own joke. I allowed them all a laugh at my expense, because even though I didn't personally know any of them, I knew that they had all been through more in their lives than I would probably ever go through in mine. When I offered to pay for the goods I had bought, he adamantly refused to accept it and sent me on my way home with a pat on my wet back that would have sent most people tumbling forward onto their faces.

On the way up the hill to my house I passed Mrs. Duffy, who was watering her award-winning rose bushes. She didn't see me and when she bent over to pick something up, she inadvertently sprayed me. I couldn't get mad for a number of reasons, most of all being the fact that I was already wet and possessed an odor that was far less than appealing.

"I'm so sorry dear," she gushed apologetically. I smiled politely and waved a hand to signal that it was alright. I continued on up the last and most unforgiving part of my journey which was a steep hill I could have done without, especially at my age and fitness level. Instead of heading straight home, I crossed the street and headed over to Rose and Tomisalv's house.

It was a small, brick house with a white, picket fence and an immaculate front lawn that was always cut so tight you could have sworn it was artificial turf from a distance. As I approached the front door, I could feel my chest tightening and my hands slickened with sweat. I knocked gently; almost too gently as I don't think that the third knock I attempted even met its intended target. Then I waited. It seemed like hours before half-a-dozen locks were undone and Rose opened the door. She was a hunched-over, apron-clad, frumpy firecracker of a woman who had perpetual dark circles around her eyes and never minced words.

"Nikola, you look tired. How was work?"

"Not bad Rose. Thank you for asking. How is Tomislav doing?"

She made the so-so gesture with her hand.

"The same."

"That's good, right?"

"I don't know. You tell me, somebody please tell me if it's good that he just lies there all day and does nothing. He's just waiting to die, that's all!" I was rendered speechless, because I knew some cheap pep-talk wasn't going to do the trick for her, especially when we're talking about a man who she had been with for over a half a century. "If you need anything, don't hesitate to call or come get me."

"I know, I won't," Rose said as she patted my arm. As I walked away, she smiled and wiped the wetness from my arm onto her apron.

"Thank you Niko."

I jogged across the street, trying to run some of the stress out of my body, but it didn't help, it just made me feel queasy, dizzy and pathetically out-of-shape. I casually walked over the piles of wood in the front yard and straight into the house, through the open doorway that was without a front door. My dad had taken the front door off of it months ago to sand it and hadn't gotten around to sanding it or putting it back up, so when I moved in I figured it was best to leave it the way it was, mostly because I didn't feel like sanding it either and had no clue how to hang a door. The funny thing was that I didn't care if anyone came into the house. There were a few semi-valuable tools lying around, but nothing that I couldn't do without. I also didn't feel like my life was valuable enough at that point to put much thought into how to secure its safety.

My dad had also torn the roof off of the house and was about to redo it right before he got the bug up his butt to hit the Internet to search for a new wife and head up into the hills. That was okay too, because I just pitched a tent that I found out in the garage and ended up basically camping inside the house that I grew up in. It was a nostalgic, painful and sometimes, in a weird way, a peaceful reminder of the journey my life had taken to eventually bring me here. I sat on a milk crate in the small living room and sipped my coffee and munched on my donut. A surge of unanticipated ambition shot through my body.

15

I got up and walked over to the bright-red rented generator that sat on the mold-infested linoleum in the tiny kitchen. I confidently fired up the generator and hooked the air hose to it. My actions felt so deliberate that I actually convinced myself that I could get something productive done. I attached the nail gun to the air hose and wouldn't you know it, the gun inadvertently shot a nail out of it that barely missed my foot and imbedded itself in the living room's hardwood floor.

With all my might I didn't do anything but gently lay the nail gun down and take a deep breath. My mind tried to quickly replay and then apply one of the book-learned relaxation techniques that I had been putting to the test over recent months without much success. I optimistically moved on to another task and hoped that things would run smoother. I grabbed the skill saw out of its plastic box and attached the to the air hose. I figured that I would cut some pieces of wood that would become part of the new entertainment center I was building.

I laid the piece of wood across my foot like I had seen the carpenters I used to work with do countless of times on the jobsites I had been on when I was selling fireplaces back in the good old days. It looked so easy when they did it, though I failed to realize that those guys did it every day for years and my foray into the construction world could easily be construed as more of a hobby than occupation. I fired up the saw and tried to cut a two-foot length off of it as it lay across the laces of my work boot. Instead of cutting anything it caught in the wood quickly and then pulled out of the wood and skipped across my foot, miraculously not cutting any of me, but leaving my steel-toed boot a sliced-up and useless mess.

I ignored all the overrated relaxation practices I had been trying to sprinkle into my life and instead turned and hurled the saw towards the back of the house. It bounced off the historic hardwood floor after taking out a nice, big chunk out of it and took one more solid bounce before flying through the glass of the back door and coming to rest in a pile of scraps in the backyard. I stormed over to the generator, clicked it off, kicked it, furiously peeled off my wet clothes, climbed into the little yellow dome tent that sat in the middle of the living room and angrily zipped it shut.

CHAPTER 5

I woke up a few hours later, but it wasn't by chance. An unpleasant and unwelcome feeling that I hadn't experienced in a long time worked its way into my gut and then slowly worked its way up my insides. I recognized it instantly because it wasn't a queasy feeling or sharp pain, it was just an overall tightening that grabbed hold and wouldn't let go. It felt like my vital organs were being put through a slowly tightening vice.

I didn't understand how it could happen again. Then the feeling suddenly disappeared. I sat in the cramped tent for a few minutes trying to see if the feeling came back, but it didn't. I discounted it as something that infiltrated my dreams and was simply playing tricks on my conscious mind. I got up slowly, went out the front door to take a look at the neighborhood and noticed a small silver scooter sitting in front of Rose and Tomislav's house. I changed into some wrinkled clothes and slowly headed across the street. When I reached the door a half-dozen locks were undone again, in the same order. Rose, still dressed as before, welcomed me with a half-hearted smile.

"How is he?"

"Not good," she said. "He won't stop crying."

I stood there, perplexed. Tomislav never cried, and I couldn't even imagine that the thought of death could bring a tear to the fifth-generation fisherman's eyes.

"Tomislav's crying?"

"No...not Tomislav! Don't be silly! It's his brother, Sasha."

I walked into the pasta-scented house and saw that Sasha was shoveling all of an awfully large pastry into his mouth as he cried uncontrollably on the couch in the cluttered, but well- kept, living room. Sasha was Tomislav's younger brother and had always lived his life in his brother's shadow. Tomislav got married and had a family. Sasha could probably count the number of dates that he went on in his life on one hand and the actual number of conversations he had with the opposite sex on less than two hands. Tomislav was a successful fisherman who had his own fleet, while Sasha always had a hard time holding down even the simplest and mundane of jobs. Tomislav had chiseled features and was a sharp dresser. Sasha was a massive man with massive, basically unattractive features who often looked like he didn't put any thought at all into what he wore out into public. Tomislav had a quick wit and smooth voice. Sasha had a significant stutter that forced him to keep his word usage to a minimum. But despite his apparent inadequacies, Sasha loved Tomislav more than anyone. And when Tomislav got sick, it was Sasha who took it the hardest.

"Hi Sasha," I said quietly.

He took a break from the eating and dusted the sugar off of his shirt and onto the floor, much to Rose's chagrin. It had been a few weeks since our paths had crossed at the house, but he approached me like we hadn't seen each other in decades. Without any warning at all he pulled me in for a hug that left me gasping violently for air.

"What have you been up to?"
"No-no-no-nothing...mmm-mmm-much," he said.

I knew he hadn't worked for years and relied on the financial support of Tomislav and Rose to pay the rent on the cracker-jack sized apartment he rented a few blocks away, but felt the need to ask what he had been up to anyhow. Just so he didn't feel left out.

"Tell him how you've been singing at the church," shouted Rose from the kitchen. Sasha fuddled with his short, chubby fingers without looking me in the eye, embarrassed by the comment from his ever-supportive sister-in-law.

"It, it, it's nothing."

"You're singing huh? That's great Sasha."

"It's j-j-just during th-th-the week. The mmm-mmm-morning mass."

"Why just during the week?"

"Because nobody is there," shouted Rose from the kitchen again. "He has such a beautiful voice, but doesn't want anyone to hear it. I don't understand it."

"I'd like to hear you sing one day Sasha, especially if you're as good as Rose says."

Sasha let a hint of a smile sneak onto his massive, pastry-crusted face before he reeled it all in and brought us all back to the reality of why we were all sitting around the house together in the first place.

"Th-th-this c-c-could be it," he said as his lips suddenly changed their shape.

"Don't talk crazy like that," I said, trying to be strong.

"Bbbbut he's just l-l-lying there n-n-not doing anything."

"He's still breathing and he's still alive."

Sasha slowly stepped away from me and wiped tears from his face.

"Tha-tha-that's true," he said calmly. "He's-s-still breathing."

I looked towards the kitchen where Rose was watching us with one eye and cooking pasta in a huge pot with the other.

"So you went in to see him?"

"Y-y-yeah, about an hour a-a-ago."

"How'd he look?"

"N-n-not sssso good," he said as he burst into tears again. Rose rolled her eyes at him as she poured boiling water from the pot into the sink.

"Niko, why don't you go see him? He would be happy to see you," she said.

I stood frozen in the living room not knowing how to answer her. I hadn't seen Tomislav in a couple of weeks, ever since he had become bedridden. He had ordered Rose not to allow anyone except the doctors to see him. And until just a couple hours ago, hadn't even let his own brother enter his bedroom.

"You sure it's okay?"

"I don't think it can hurt, he's just been sleeping most of the time."

"I'm not sure that I can--," I blurted out before she cut me off mid-sentence.

"It's the second door on the right," she said with an air of insistence that I refused, mostly out of fear, to resist.

Sasha had gone back to the couch and was shoveling more food into his mouth as I slowly headed down the short, narrow hallway. As I took unusually short steps and quick, but quiet breathes, I wondered what he was going to look like.

I wondered if he still had his famous lamb-chop sideburns and any of his already-thinned hair. I wondered if he still had his tan or if his skin had turned to the color of ghosts. I wondered if the whites of his eyes were still white, or had already turned yellow. But none of my hypothesizing mattered the minute I opened the door to his room, because he wasn't there.

CHAPTER 6

His room was simple with only a bed, nightstand, dresser and closet-sized bathroom in it. It wasn't hard to figure out that he wasn't there. I went around his bed to see if he had fallen off of it, but he hadn't. I checked the tiny bathroom then looked under the bed for some unknown reason and even behind the door to see if was playing some type of sick joke on me. He wasn't.

I inspected his dresser, looking for a clue. A wooden, hand-made box was sitting open on top of the three-drawer dresser. Inside of the box was a well-worn, but attractive watch. Though I usually wasn't one to snoop, the mystery of the moment swept me up. I gently picked it up out of the case and inspected it. It was heavier than it looked; a compliment to the sturdy workmanship of years past. I felt the worn, sweat-stained brown leather band in my fingers. I turned it over and looked at the back of the watch. There was something engraved in it. It read..."1959 U.S. Open Cup Champions."

I held the watch in my hands and looked over Tomislav's belongings on the top of the dresser. There was the box, a black plastic comb, folded up handkerchief and a framed photo. It was a black and white photo of him amongst a celebratory group of his teammates. He was in the middle of all of them, holding the trophy triumphantly with both hands in front of his face as he planted a big kiss on it. I knew that years ago he had led a local team of fishermen, boat builders and longshoremen to the town's first and only Open Cup Championship, which was the oldest soccer tournament in the country.

23

I never saw him play, his career had long ended before I was even born, but heard from the other old-school guys that even on my best day he would have spun me into the ground with his dribbling exploits. The moment took me back to better days and I found myself in a daze while I reminisced about how cool it would have been to be Tomislav at that moment, kissing the most prestigious soccer trophy in the nation.

My daydream was rudely interrupted by the thought of what I was going to tell Rose when I got back into the living room. I propped the photo back on the dresser and gently put the watch back in its case. I closed the bedroom door quietly behind me and walked out into the living room. Rose was sitting with Sasha on the couch, gently stroking his hair as he calmly continued to eat pastries while he rested his head in her apron-clad lap.

"What is it Niko?"

I still wasn't sure how to say it, so I just said it. But it came out wrong anyway.

"He's gone."

Rose threw her hands into the air so hard that I thought the roof was going to lift off the house.

Then she wailed something in her native tongue.

"No, no. He's not dead," I injected quickly. "He's not dead! He's just not in his bedroom." Rose gathered herself quickly and studied my face for more to the story. There wasn't any. She pulled Sasha's massive head off of her lap and sprung to her feet. She approached me cautiously with a furrowed brow.

"It's no possible" she said.

"It is possible, go look for yourself."

The Gift of Stoppage Time

She hurried down the hall in short, choppy steps that had to wear her shoes out by the week. There was no knock on the door. She flung the door open so hard that if Tomislav had been on the other side of it, he would have been knocked into the afterlife whether or not it was even supposed to be his time to go.

"Tomislav, Tomislav!" She hollered to what was simply an empty room. She ran into the hall and looked back my way. There was a look in her eyes that I hadn't seen before. It wasn't a look of shock or anger or sadness or joy. It was just a look of pure confusion, which probably felt worse to her considering how much she had been going through the last few months. There was no way for her to expect any of this. It was supposed to be painful and gut-wrenching, but not confusing. There was no way to know how to react to the situation. She ran down the hall and into the backyard. Then I heard her voice again. The whole neighborhood heard her voice again.

"Tomislav, what are you doing?"

I wanted to respect her privacy as she searched for her missing-in-house husband, but also felt the need to keep an eye on her to make sure that she was okay. I raced down the hall and looked through the window in the back door. Sure enough, he was there. He was sitting on the back step, casually smoking a cigarette in his tank top and tattered boxer shorts. He actually looked better than I thought he would even though I only saw the side of his face. It didn't seem like Rose cared how good he looked at the moment. She tried to interrogate him, but he wasn't having any of it.

"When did you get up?"

"Shhh, please Rose. Let me enjoy my cigarette," he asked of her quietly and politely.

"You shouldn't be smoking," she said.

"Why not, will it kill me?"

"Don't be funny with me," she said. "How do you feel?"

Tomislav took a long look at his cigarette and slowly nodded his head to a rhythm unheard by Rose and me. He lifted his face to capture the afternoon sun as he took a quick hit of his cigarette.

"I actually feel pretty good," he said.

Rose stood there with her hands on her hips as she tried to figure out if she was really having the conversation that she was having. I smiled through the doorway, and wondered as much as anyone else, what the heck was going to happen next. Rose continued on her quest for information from him, but changed tactics from interrogating him, to simply talking to him like it was any other day of the week.

"Do you want something to eat?"

"Sure, why not? But I am in a hurry."

"What? Hurry? Why?"

"I'm going to watch futbol, like every Sunday."

"What are you talking about?! Where are you going? You are in no shape to go out," bellowed Rose.

"I go to the soccer game like every week. Me and the guys, we always meet for the game. You know that," he said. Tomislav sounded slightly exacerbated and annoyed all at the same time. He snuffed out his cigarette with a succession of deliberate taps on the edge of the concrete step and slowly rose to his feet.

Rose tried to grab his arm to hold him up, but he defiantly yet gently redirected it away. Not wanting to get caught eavesdropping, I quickly turned away from the window to run back into the living room. Instead of turning sharply and making the short gallop back into the living room, I clumsily clipped my own heels together, an act that sent me tumbling to the unforgiving floor. I scrambled to my feet, ignoring the stabbing pain that suddenly infiltrated my elbow and limped into the living room where Sasha was sitting quietly with a piece of pastry resting on his protruding belly.

"D-d-did you find him?"

"He's in the backyard."

"What's he ddd-doing?"

"He was having a cigarette."

"H-h-having a cigarette?"

"Yeah."

"W-w-what's he doing n-n-now?"

"Getting ready to go to a soccer game."

Sasha gave me an odd look for a minute. I could tell that he wasn't buying my account of the story and was probably thinking that it was, in fact, just a story that I made up. As he rose to his feet, he sent a bunch of the pasty down his already stain-riddled shirt.

"W-w-what game...and w-with who?"

"A game that doesn't exist...and apparently with you," I said solemnly. Suddenly Rose shuffled into the room all out of breath. Her face was flush, like she had just seen a ghost. Her hands trembled as she grabbed for my arm. "What are we going to do Nikola? The doctors said that he would never get out of bed, but now he is out of bed and he wants to go out.

27

What do I do?" I could tell that they were both freaked out. Sasha started to sway a little bit, like he was about to pass out. He said four words before his massive kneecaps gave way.

"W-w-why is this h-h-happening?" I took two quick steps towards him, hoping to catch him in time before his two-hundred and fifty pound body hit the hardwood. I reached him in time, but he was much too large of a man for me to hold up. I fell with him and cushioned his fall a little bit with my own body. It didn't feel good, but I was glad that he didn't hurt himself. He awoke instantly when we hit the ground. He laid there wide-eyed next to me and was still waiting for an answer to his pre-pass out question.

"I don't know why this is happening," I answered. I had to lie.

"M-m-maybe it's a mm-m-miracle," he proclaimed optimistically.
I got up and Rose gripped my arm even harder than before, so hard I almost snapped it away from her out of pure reflex. Her mind was racing at the speed of light and I didn't blame her one bit for it. I went through the same thing.

"Could it be a miracle? Do you think that Tomi is snapping out of it?" What was happening was miraculous; I had seen it firsthand many years ago with my mom. But it wasn't the type of miracle that they wanted.
I paused and made sure that I chose my words carefully. They came out wrong yet again. My honesty couldn't be questioned, but my tact waned.

"I don't think that you just snap-out of cancer," I said.

I saw the air empty out of both of them and knew that I was the culprit with the needle.

Rose let go of my arm and took a seat in what was usually Tomislav's reliable recliner.

Sasha slumped down in the sofa again and magically made a handful of pastry disappear. There was a long silence as everyone in the room except me, tried to figure out what was going on with their beloved family member. Rose held her forehead tightly with her hand as she fished for more information on the inexplicable event involving her husband that we were caught in the middle of.

"What is it then Niko, what make him get up?"

Even though I was pretty sure that I knew what was going on, I didn't feel like I could tell them yet. Because I cared for them so deeply, I wouldn't tell them yet.

"I don't think it's important to figure out why he's up right now."

"Then what is important?" Rose got up from the chair and gazed down the hallway.

"What's important now is to figure out what to do with him next."

Rose waved me off and then shuffled down the hallway and listened into the bedroom. Seconds later, she shuffled back to us, out of breath and more flustered than before.

"He is in the shower!"

"He's really serious about this going out thing," I said as I thought out loud.

"He isn't in any shape to go out," said an infuriated Rose in an adamant whisper.

"W-w-we should c-c-call his doctor," offered Sasha logically.

"We should call his doctor," reiterated Rose.

I knew I couldn't tell them what was really happening with Tomislav, but I also knew that calling the doctor was a total waste of time. The doctors didn't even have an answer for what was going on with him.

"Doctors will probably just tell us to get him into bed again," I offered honestly.

"He won't get into bed, not the way he is acting now," said Rose.

"W-w-we should call an amb-am-ambulance."

I paced the living room, carefully thinking out my words and trying to hold my emotions in check. I couldn't fall apart in front of them no matter how much I wanted to. Seeing Tomislav suffer had been eating me up inside for months. He had been a great friend, bodyguard on occasion and a father figure to me for years. I didn't want him to go as much as anyone else, but I also was mature enough and experienced enough to accept the harsh, brutal reality of his situation.

"He really wants to go to a soccer game," I said. "So maybe we just take him to a game."

Rose stormed back in from the kitchen where she had wandered off to seconds earlier. "What game? Nobody plays in town anymore! It's been years since he went to a game."

"I know, I know. But maybe I can put something together."

Sasha just sat there shaking his head. "W-w-we need to get him to a h-h-hospital," he mumbled under his breath over and over again.

"I don't even understand what you are trying to do," Rose said. "He's already in the shower."

"I'll make some calls and try to put together a game at Daniel's Field for him to go to."

"But that isn't possible."

"I don't know what else to do Rose. He is up and wants to go to a soccer game, why don't we try to give him what he wants. What's the worst that could happen?"

We all looked around the room at each other and knew what the worse that could happen to him was and prior to him getting up we were all prepared for it. But now it was the furthest thing on everyone's mind, except mine. I started sweating profusely, and since I never wore a watch I couldn't even look to see how unreasonable the task I was undertaking actually was. I could see that even though there was plenty of daylight left the chances of making anything like a game happen out of nowhere were slim to none, but I didn't care. I laid a confident hand on Rose's shoulder.

"Cook him a nice, early dinner that takes a long time to eat and I will see what I can do."

"D-D-D Dessert too?"

"Absolutely Sasha" I said as I gently closed the front door behind me and sprinted down their front steps with my stomach tied in knots that not even the strongest man in the world could undo.

CHAPTER 7

I raced to the closet-sized, half-finished bathroom just in time to throw-up my cold pizza lunch into the brand-new toilet I had just installed. Once wasn't enough however, and my stomach forced me to volunteer my lunch to the toilet again and again to equal three times total. I stood up and toweled-off my sweat drenched head and face. A thousand painful moments paraded through my head with only a fraction of them actually involving Tomislav. My stomach tightened again and I was forced to wheel around to the toilet once more. I wanted to cry but was too tired. I wanted to put my fist through a door like I used to, but didn't want to ruin my own handy work around the house.

I pulled my ragged body up again and went to look at myself in the mirror another time when I noticed a body behind me. I spun around as quick as I could, fist clenched and ready for action. My beleaguered fist was grabbed by the intruder without much fanfare.

"Keep wishing little brother."

"I do have a doorbell that works."

"Yes, that is true. But you don't have a door." My big brother Frank and I always had a typical love-hate relationship. We were always just too competitive not to be threatened by the others' successes. He was a very good wrestler who never understood soccer until recently and I was a very good soccer player who never understood his sport of choice.

His body was constructed by an engineer, not created by an artist like mine. All his proportions were sharp and obtrusive, where mine were more fluid, lean and smoothly rounded. His hair was cropped short, his body hair shaved and his eyes small and perpetually squinted, like he was always unhappy about something. He never left town and never wanted to. Instead, he stayed around and was now the Athletic Director at our old high school. He loved being the big fish in the little pond. Since he towered over all his students and looked like he could crush them in one fell swoop, his authority was seldom questioned, which was something he loved as he got deeper and deeper into compliment-starved adulthood.

We saw each other when we had to, not really when we wanted to. He never supported me growing up and for spite, I never supported him. Our mom used to negotiate all household truces between the two of us, and once she left us, it was no holds barred. We used to get into it pretty good and things evened out over time because even though he was bigger than me, I was much more agile and fit.

"What do you have...another midday hangover?"

"No," I said.

"Then what is your deal?"

"Shouldn't you still be at school or something?" I snorted.

"The students had a half day. I was supposed to be in a seminar, but I blew it off. I figured that I would come over to see how my little brother was doing on his little project."

I turned and inspected his insincere face. His smirk intentionally gave away his weak attempt at sarcasm.

"Good, because I need one to," I said as I escorted him out of the cramped bathroom and into the living room. We both pulled milk crates underneath us and sat just inside the open doorway so that the cool afternoon breeze hit us ever-so-slightly. I would have offered him a beer if I had one, but I didn't. It made what would have been a very forced hospitable portion of the visit much less complicated.

"You remember Tomislav, don't you?"

"Sure...yes, I do."

"Well, you know that he's been sick for a while now, with cancer."

"No I did not know that."

"Yeah, well he had cancer for a real long time. It wasn't getting better or worse, he was just living with it. Then it suddenly started getting way worse... like all of the sudden. But he was so sick of all the medication that he had been on for all the years that he told the doctors he didn't want to take any medications anymore."

"He wanted to die," said Frank.

"No, no, he just didn't want to live the way he felt like he did when he was on the medication. I remember he told me that it made his life seem distant, like he was watching it all on television, like it wasn't real. And even though it helped with the pain, he didn't like feeling different. He used to say it made him feel like he wasn't himself anymore, and he hated it."

"So he was willing to die if he could be himself until he died?"

"Basically...yeah. He's an old-school guy. They can be stubborn. But there's no gray area with those guys, it's either this way or that way and they don't mess around."

"What happened when he stopped the medication?"

"He just kept living pretty well for a while, and then it got worse and the pain got to be so much that he let them put him back on the medication again. So he's just been basically bedridden for the last few weeks and he wouldn't let anyone go see him."

"That is too bad."

"So he's just been lying there...all doped up...waiting to die."

"He die?"

"No. In fact...he's up."

"Up?"

"Yeah, like up and in the shower now, thinking he's going to a soccer game."

"How did that happen?"

"You remember with mom right? She went through something similar."

My big brother got up off the milk crate slowly and went over to the power drill. He picked it up and revved it once, lost in some heavy thoughts he wasn't too interested in bringing back on a glorious winter afternoon.

"Do you think that is what is happening to him?"

"It's got to be, how else do you explain it? I mean, he just got up. No warning at all. He just got up, and now wants to go to a soccer game."

"That is crazy. Mom didn't do anything like that."

"Her body was just so ravaged by it. But she was calling out for us and talking more than she had in months in her last hours," I said.

"Yes, I remember. That was weird," he said as he sat back down and stared at the floor. "Does his family know what is going on?"

"No, they think it's a miracle."

My brother just shook his head as he stared blankly at the freshly-sanded wood floor beneath him.

"Are you going to tell them?"

"It would break their hearts."

"But you have to tell them."

"Yeah, I know I do. But not yet."

What I needed from my brother was for his soccer team to be ready to play a soccer game in a few short hours. It killed me to ask for a couple of reasons. First of all, his team was awful. It was a group of teachers that got together mostly so that they could get fit enough to have a chance to ask some of the hotter teachers at work out on dates. And secondly, I didn't want to owe him any more than I needed to, which at this point was nothing.

"So what's the favor?" he asked.

"You know that team you play for?"

"Sure."

"You think they'd want to play a game under the lights at Daniel's Field?" He crinkled a brow and gave me a suspicious once-over as he inspected my face for sincerity.

"I figured if Tomislav wants a soccer game to go to, I might as well try to put one together for him."

"That might be some pretty ambitious thinking."

I dropped my head in a moment of defeat, but pulled it together enough to keep the conversation headed in the right direction.

"It might be, but what else do you recommend I do?"

My brother tapped his foot on the wood floor for a moment.

"Even if I do get my team to play, who are we going to play against?"

36

"I'll figure something out. I just need to know if you can get your team together in a few hours, I don't have much time on this. Can I count on you?"

"I'll make some calls."

"Oh yeah, what was the favor you came over to ask me?"

"I was going to see if you would paint my house for some beers since you're apparently Mr. Handyman nowadays.

But I think I might just ask you to play for my team instead," he said with a sinister smile.

A sharp pain ran from the back of my head to just above my eyebrows and back again. I hadn't played organized soccer in years and if I were to ever get back into the game again; my brother's team would have been the last group I would have wanted to contribute my talents to. But my choices were limited and I needed teams, so I relented. It hurt a lot, but I did think it would be fun to yell at my goalkeeper brother every time he let one get by him.

"What about my Achilles injury?"

"You hurt that thing years ago, get over it. It's the unwanted weight gain I would be worried about if I were you," he said sarcastically.

"Yeah, but I still feel a twinge in it from time to time."

"That twinge is all in your head. You had better get over it, because you will be our center midfielder."

"My debut won't be tonight though, I've got to stay with Tomislav."

"Fine, but you are mine when our season starts in a few weeks."

"Whatever...just don't leak it to the press yet."

"I will call you in a bit to let you know the status of the boys," he said as he cruised out of the house and into the fading daylight.

CHAPTER 8

The pressure of running out of time was not a new feeling to me. I had felt it ever since my mom died in the middle of my senior year when I was seventeen years old. I went from counting up the days until adulthood, to counting down the days until I too, would die. It wasn't a feeling I enjoyed or welcomed. In fact, after she died, there were many nights where I thought that I was going to die too. There was no rhyme or reason to it. I wasn't sick. I just thought that I might die and every night, for a very long time after the cancer finally devoured the last bit of her organs I would go to sleep seriously wondering if I was going to wake up in the morning. Seeing death up close and personal made it too real to avoid. I knew, because I had seen it firsthand, that it would get me one day.

The funny thing was that it seemed more logical that after seeing how fragile life was that I would kick butt doing things with every minute of life that I was gifted. But seeing somebody run out of time had the opposite effect on me. I couldn't focus on any one-thing. The more time I had, the less I did with it.

I ran out of motivation quickly and would move onto something else without ever really completing or accomplishing much. I never fully committed to anything. If I didn't love it, it wouldn't hurt to lose it, I thought. Time wasn't an enemy, it was simply a non-factor. Instead of using it wisely, I just went through my life wasting it. But there was something different about wanting to help Tomislav. I did learn about what was happening to him from my mom's death. His family couldn't and wouldn't want to accept what was happening even if I told them, so I didn't bother to. The most important thing was to get a game set up so that he could get out and experience what I knew was going to be the last night of his life.

CHAPTER 9

Without a clock in sight, I stood in the door-less doorway and looked out over the harbor as the sun worked its way down into the far-off horizon. It was truly a beautiful winter day, a day that didn't look interested in taking anybody's life. But I knew that things didn't work that way. People died on beautiful days all the time. I just hoped that today would be different. My hope was overshadowed by what I knew to be fact and that was that Tomislav was going through a very unique time in his life and I was going to make sure that I was a critical part of making it special for him.

I got into a cold shower since I hadn't fixed that water heater yet. It seemed to help get the blood flowing, but the stress was mounting and I had to figure out a way to keep myself relaxed because if I looked like a wreck when I saw Tomislav he would definitely know that something was up.

I got dressed into some jeans and a t-shirt and ran back across the street, my stomach still in an untie-able knot. I knocked on the door harder and more deliberately than before.

The locks were undone almost simultaneously as Rose must have been watching for my appearance through the window.

The door flung open. She suddenly had a look of horror on her face. I wondered if something happened to Tomislav. Before I could even ask, she blurted out what her face was trying to say.

"Where is your suit!?"

I was dumbfounded.

41

"My suit?"

"Yes Niko, your suit."

"I don't have a suit."

"You must have a suit Niko! Tomi always wore a suit to the games. And your face, what is wrong with your face?"

I reached for my face wondering what she was talking about.

"I don't know...what?"

"You must shave Niko! And you must wear a suit! Go now, hurry. He is almost ready!"

I stormed back to the house, cussing myself. I had no clue what I was going to do as far as the suit was concerned, so I started shaving quickly. I was interrupted by the phone. It was my brother.

"My team is ready to rock and roll. Do we have access to the locker rooms?"

"Absolutely."

"Do you really have the stadium for tonight?"

"I'm working on it, but it shouldn't be a problem."

It reminded me that I hadn't even bothered to call Cowboy Chris to see if getting the stadium on such short notice was something he could help me out with.

"I need another favor."

"What is it little brother?"

"Do you have a suit that I could borrow?"

"A suit? What do you need a suit for?"

"Tomislav used to always get dressed up for the games and his wife wants me to get dressed up too."

"It's going to cost you."

"What now?" I cringed as I waited for his next demand.

"I need a new varsity soccer coach at the high school."

"You know I can't commit to that!"

"Why the heck not? You're gypsy days are over with. You are here for good little brother and there is nothing wrong with that. Now commit to your alma mater and bring us a championship like you did when you were a player."

My options were not only running low, I didn't have any.

"Fine...just get the suit over here."

"I will be back over in a few minutes coach."

CHAPTER 10

The suit that my brother brought over wasn't a suit at all. It was a tuxedo. And it was white. But I was out of options and running low on time and I figured that it was better than nothing. It fit poorly and smelled funky since he hadn't worn it since his wedding day which was ten years ago. My brother was going on nine and a half years of being divorced. The fact that his marriage lasted half a year never seemed to surprise anyone, least of all me.

I scrambled through my phone book and called every guy I could from the old days as I tried to scrounge up another team for my brother's talent-deficient team of weekend warriors to play. I was forced to leave a lot of messages, but did get a hold of a couple live voices. A former high school teammate who was nothing more than a glorified equipment manager was heavily involved in an online gaming tournament and wouldn't leave his computer. Another guy who used to own a soccer shop in town said that he would have played if he hadn't doubled his body weight since his playing days and was now even having a hard time getting off the couch to reach the refrigerator in time for another unneeded snack.

Maybe I should have never told them the game was going to be played in a stadium, under the lights. It might have scared them off. Never mind the fact that the amount of spectators probably could have been counted on one hand. I sat in my unsettled living room wondering if what I had gotten myself into was another destined-to-fail challenge that I never should have put myself up to in the first place. A dozen little failures and a handful of big ones raced through my mind that made my temples throb and my palms sweat.

44

Then a thought crossed my mind that seemed so far-fetched and improbable that it ran along the same company line that the whole night was shaping up like. So I grabbed the old hand-painted orange strand-cruiser that had been left on the side yard and headed down the steep street towards the harbor. The daylight was fading and I was getting concerned by the lack of time I had left to put the game together, but what could I do? I knew as well as anyone that I was running out of time. I didn't need to be reminded by anybody or anything.

The ride down to the Recreation Center was easy, but getting back up the hill to my house was going to be another thing altogether. I didn't let it bother me as there were many more pressing issues for me to tend to.

There were a few guys hanging around the front door of the club that looked none too pleased by my sweaty, disheveled appearance.

"Is Mr. Nowinski around?"

A miniature-looking teen who sported a nasty scowl nodded me inside. I entered the game room area of the sprawling recreation center and treaded cautiously through the raucous crowd of teenagers who engaged in healthy bouts of trash-talking as they hunched over air-hockey games, pool tables and video games.

A door from the gym flung open and in rolled Mr. Nowinski, followed by a handful of sweaty kids who had obviously been involved in a spirited game of something out on the hardwood. He recognized me right away. He bellowed out a welcome in his trademark booming bark that he had patented from decades of teaching over-energized kids the finer points of all sports.

"Look who's back in town!"

"I've been back for a while now Mr. Nowinski."

"And you're just now getting around to visiting me?"

"Yeah, I know. It's bad...I have no excuse."

He rolled his wheelchair up alongside me and gave me a brisk slap to my gut.

"You look like you've put on a little weight there."

"The days of burning it all off on the field are over. Now all I do is pack it on."

"I heard that," he said as he patted his own mildly protruding belly. "But I've got a few years on you kid."

"That's an understatement."

"Hey now...let's not get cruel."

We went into his office. The kids that had been following him out of the gym scattered in every direction. He leaned forward with a big smile on his face and interlocked his fingers on his paper-strewn desk.

"How's everything going for you Niko?"

"Well, I feel kind of bad asking you this, since we haven't see each other in so long, but I'm sort of in a bind."

"What is it? You need some money? You're not on drugs are you?"

"No, no...I'm okay. But do you happen to remember Tomislav? He was the older guy who always used to be at the games at Daniel's? He always used to lean against the fence right under the clubhouse?"

Mr. Nowinski leaned back in his wheelchair and interlocked his fingers behind his head as he reached back in time.

"Yeah, yeah, I think I do. I used to hang out with him during the games sometimes. Real tan, serious-looking guy?"

"That's him."

"He sure used to love watching you play. He always used to say that you played the game the way it was supposed to be played...with a lot of heart."

I kept my emotions in tact as Mr. Nowinski took me back to the good old days when Tomislav used to show me how to survive games in one of the most brutal soccer leagues in the country.

"Well, to make a long story short. He had been struggling with cancer for a while. But a funny thing happened earlier today. He just got up out of bed and now wants to go to Daniel's Field to watch a soccer game."

Mr. Nowinski's eyes roamed the room that was filled with multiple trophies from his many years as Director of the Rec Center.

"Why does he want to do that?"

"Because that's what he used to do."

"But nobody plays soccer there anymore."

"I know. So what I offered to do was to try and put together a game for him to go to." Mr. Nowinski shook his head and let out a little laugh.

"How are you going to do that?"

"My brother plays for a pretty bad Men's League team and he offered to bring them down, so he's been running around trying to round all his guys up. And I was hoping that you had some kids around here who might want to get a game tonight."

"Tonight?"

"Yeah, like in a couple of hours," I said optimistically.

47

Mr. Nowinski wheeled back around his desk and led me into the hallway. We both scanned the room full of teenagers of all shapes and sizes.

"I know a few of them play soccer in the gym from time to time. I'll see what I can do."

"That would be awesome."

"They probably don't have any gear though."

"I'll scrounge some up for them. Tell them not to worry about it."

I slapped him on the back affectionately and started down the hall with some welcomed confidence.

"They're going to want to keep the gear, just so you know," he said as he negotiated the sweetest deal he could for his boys.

"It's all theirs if they show up."

"Oh...they'll be there."

CHAPTER 11

Before I got too far up the lung-crushing hill that led to the house on my orange bike, Cowboy Chris bailed me out. He pulled up to me in his truck and dumped my ancient ride into the back. I was glad that he helped make the "climb" of death more like the stairway to heaven, because the evening was still young and I could already tell that I was going to need all the energy I could muster for the events that lie ahead.

We pulled up onto the front yard of my house and Cowboy Chris parked his truck with the front axle perched up on a stack of wood, just to show that his truck was capable of doing it. It didn't bother me at all that he was showing off, because I honestly didn't know who he was showing off for. If it made him feel better, I was all for it.

I took a quick glance across the street at Tomislav and Rose's house and noticed what looked like a non-descript rental-type car parked in front of it. I did a double-take at it as I walked through the open doorway with Cowboy Chris, who was sporting a six-pack tucked firmly underneath his arm. We got into the house and he immediately grabbed a milk crate and sat down on it while he simultaneously popped the cap off his bottle of beer with his teeth.

Then he offered me one. I took it and sipped from it as I hoped that it would quell the nerves that were growing in my stomach.

"How's it been goin' pardner?"

"Not bad, what's up with you?" Cowboy Chris caught something out of the corner of his eye and shot to his feet.

"Not a lot pardner...what the heck is that?"

"A tuxedo."

"I know that. What's it doin' here?"

"It's my outfit for the evening."

"To where...the prom? Ya got a date for the prom that ya ain't tellin' me about pardner?" I chugged the rest of my beer as he went over to the tux that was hanging on the door to the unused and empty master bedroom. It looked way too big and smelled like old-outdated musty cologne.

"No, it's for a soccer game."

"Pretty formal for a soccer game pardner. Don't ya think?"

"Yeah, but it's for an old-timer that used to get all dressed up for the games down at Daniel's Field." Cowboy Chris rubbed the stubble on his face as he looked the hanging tuxedo up and down.

"He's going to wear this tuxedo pardner?"

"No...I am."

"Why would ya do that?" I walked over and stood next to Cowboy Chris in front of the hanging tuxedo. I hadn't worn a tuxedo since Senior Prom. At my brother's wedding, I just wore a sweater because I wasn't even in it. I was glad that our relationship had gotten a little better and that I was actually able to rely on my brother to provide me with a team for the game even though he was extorting the heck out of me.

"I'm wearing it out of respect. He's doing it, so I'm doing it."

"He's wearin' a tux too?"

"No, but this is the best I could come up with."

"You're gonna look damn silly in that pardner."

I was frustrated that Cowboy Chris was missing the point, so I jumped right into the nuts and bolts of the situation.

"Tomislav has been real sick for a long time. He somehow managed to get up today after being bedridden for weeks. Now he's up and wants to go to a soccer game. I offered to get a game together for him and am now scrambling to make it happen."

"Ya sure look like you're scramblin' pardner."

"I'm just trying to figure out my next step."

"So what's your next step pardner?" Luckily, he walked right into it, so it made the transition into the request pretty painless.

"My next step is to get Daniel's Field for the night."

"Really...now?"

"Yeah. Is that something you think you can help me with?"

I knew Cowboy Chris liked it when people needed his help. I also knew that he took his own sweet time deciding who and when to help. He deliberately slowed down his sip of beer. Then he cruised around the living room at snail's pace, relishing the fact that his services were now needed. I had heard that his demands in return could be pretty involved if he didn't like you.

"I gotta friend who works for the City that owes me a favor."

"So you think you can make it happen?"

"Think so. Get your game on pardner."

"Not me...no way! I'm just organizing this thing."

"You're not gonna play tonight pardner?"

"Nope."

"You're tellin' me that you're just gonna watch?"

"That's right."

"I reckon I might just have to call ya a liar on that one pardner. Would you be willin' to put a little money on that?"

"Sure, how much?"

"Hundred bucks."

I knew I wasn't really in any position to spare a hundred bucks, but figured that since I ultimately controlled the bet that the risk was worth taking.

"You're on!"

He patted my back and started to walk out the front doorway, but then turned back to me and pointed a confident finger at me.

"See you down there in a couple of hours."

Cowboy Chris dialed his cell phone as he walked out my front doorway and into evening sky. Suddenly, he was unapologetically bumped and almost knocked on his butt by just over a hundred pounds, of pure rage.

"This is all going to be on you...you know that, don't you?"

I was shocked to see her. It had been years since we saw each other last.

"Where did you come from?"

"Don't worry about it Mr. Fix-it. What the hell do you think you're doing!" She screamed in my face loud enough for everyone in the neighborhood to hear.

"About what?"

She stepped into me and delivered a two-handed push to the chest that sent me reeling back. There was nothing flirtatious about it at all. That bummed me out.

"About my dad! How is taking him out to a soccer game going to help?" I straightened my shirt and made sure that I was more than an arms length away from her.

"How's it going to hurt?"

She was left speechless for a moment. She turned her attention to Chris who has leaning in the doorway. He tipped his hat to her.

"Howdy Angela?"

She ignored his hello, but did snag the last beer of his six-pack. She took a swig so healthy that it would have made any frat boy proud.

"You're welcome," he said sarcastically. She pretended to not hear him as she continued her verbal assault on me. She took a deep breath and lowered her voice as she tried to change tactics on me. "We need to get him to a hospital Niko," she said as calmly as she possibly could. I saw that her face was getting redder and redder as she uttered the words. I walked over to Cowboy Chris and grabbed the beer he was drinking. He gave it up without much of a fight. He was just happy to have the best seat in the house. I wasn't about to let her just waltz into town and start calling the shots.

"How's taking him out going to hurt? And how is taking to him a hospital going to help?" I asked her. She paced the room in front of me with her fists clenched on both sides. I knew she wasn't going to try to hit me in front of Chris, but I did remember how pissed she got when I told her that I never wanted us to be officially together way back when we were in high school. She had a slight build, but she had a temper. I also remember when she found out that I was dating a little sophomore after I stupidly let her go packing. I got shouted down pretty good on the phone for over an hour on that. But looking back, I deserved every bit of it. She was just trying to keep me from making the biggest mistake of my life. Even with her help, I screwed it all up. She came over to me and laid a soft hand on my shoulder.

"Niko, I know where this is all coming from and I know that you think you're just trying to help and I admire your effort. But he's my dad, not yours, and I am determined to get him to a hospital where they can help him," she said in a patronizing tone. "What game is it anyway?"

I slugged some beer and watched Cowboy Chris slowly slink outside. "It's a game I'm putting together right now." She looked over to where Cowboy Chris was standing then wheeled around back at me. She grabbed my shirt and pulled me into her. Her eyes were usually a deep brown, but had suddenly turned a fire-engine red. I knew that most of her anger had nothing to do with me, or at least I hoped that it didn't. She let the volume of her voice raise to its highest level.

"So, there's not even a real game to go to? I figured as much! And what are you going to do with my dad if there's no game for him to watch?"

"I'm not—."

She let go of my shirt and pushed herself away from me. She made absolutely no efforts to disguise her disgust with me and my idea.

"I'm sure that more disappointment is just what he needs right now." I could see all the pain in her face. Her olive-colored skin was tightened, her thin neck muscles taught. Her eyes fired red and then got extinguished with tear-drop rain as she screamed at me. I resented the fact that she thought she could waltz into town and become the expert on what to do with her sick dad after not seeing him for years, even though he was her dad and not mine.

I also couldn't let go of a comment she made towards me at the beginning of her tirade. I felt it was mine turn to interrogate her.

"Where do you think this is all coming from?" I asked her.

She picked up her beer off the floor and drank the rest of what hadn't spilled out. Cowboy Chris had come back into the house and was standing at the doorway again with one of his feet propped up on a milk crate. He gave me a wink, like he thought all the drama unfolding in front of him was cool. I didn't think it was at all. It was too real to be cool, something Cowboy Chris didn't understand. It was something he couldn't understand unless he knew the entire history of Angela and I and our situation, or lack thereof over the years. Angela never liked to be on the receiving end of pointed questions and she certainly hadn't changed in the amount of time since I had seen her last.

"What?"

"Where do you think this is all coming from? You said that you knew where all of this was coming from? Where's that?" I asked her.

She stole a milk crate from under Cowboy Chris' foot and sat down on it.

"It's coming from your mom's whole deal," she said.

"My mom's deal?"

"I was there remember? That was, until you dumped me for that little stupid sophomore. Please don't use my dad's situation to help you ease your guilt over your mom." I spiked my empty beer can into the hardwood floor that was going to have to be finished again anyway.

"That has nothing to do with it! I'm simply trying to help your dad enjoy whatever time he has left on this planet. Your dad has been a good friend of mine for years, and has helped me out a lot. I just want to be there to help him...that's all." Angela stepped into the doorway next to Cowboy Chris and leaned onto the other side of it.

"It could be a miracle," she said.

"It could be."

"But you don't think it is."

I ran a heavy hand through my hair and looked over to Chris hoping he had another beer for me or at least some good advice. He just shrugged back at me, failing on both fronts.

"I don't know what to think right now."

"He wasn't even happy to see me."

"You've been gone a long time, he was probably just surprised."

Angela walked slowly over to me and lowered her voice as she spoke. I knew the conversation sucked, but I couldn't get over how good it was to see her again.

"I need to get him to a hospital. Niko, will you help me convince my mom of that?" Even the surprised sight of my lost love couldn't get me to change my mind about helping Tomislav enjoy the night. I couldn't crack under the pressure. It was only the beginning of what was to be many pressures of the night, and I wasn't going to give in that easily, at least not this early in the evening.

"No Angela, I won't try to talk your mom out of it. I think that it's important to give your dad what he wants right now. And what he wants is to spend time outside at a soccer game with his friends...and to live a little bit. You know, he hasn't really had the chance to do that lately."

"Don't rub it in," she snapped.

"I'm not trying to rub it in. I'm just pointing out the fact that you haven't been around to see how bad he's been feeling lately."

"So you're telling me that this is all about him? It has nothing to do with you?" She cast a steely-eyed stare at me as she tried valiantly to poke holes in the sincerity of my actions.

"Yeah."

She delivered another push to my chest that caught me off-balance and sent me tumbling onto the unforgiving hard-wood floor. Cowboy Chris started to laugh until he realized there was nothing funny about that fact that I was just assaulted.

"That's a bunch of B.S. and you know it!" She stood over me for a second and glared down at me. She was as angry as I ever remember her. Cowboy Chris directed a question at her on her way out that only made matters worse.

"Are ya still married Angela?"

"No, you jerk! I just got divorced a few months ago," she said as she slapped him across the bicep on her way out. Chris gave me the "thumbs up" as I lay on the ground, making sure that she was gone. Then I sprung to my feet and stood in the doorway watched her run down the steep street and around the corner. "That went well," said Cowboy Chris sarcastically.

"Compared to some of the conversations we've had in the past...it did," I said as I let out a little laugh of defeat. I sat down on the front porch steps and gazed down on the bright lights of harbor. I knew that Angela had somewhere to go, she had always been resourceful. She wasn't going to spend the rest of the night wandering the streets. Even though her tongue-lashing hurt a little bit, I could relate to that reeling feeling of everything being out of control. Seeing her that way for the first time in years bummed me out the more I thought about it.

We went to different elementary schools in town and didn't meet until her family moved in across the street from us the summer before high school. She already had swarms of guys at her beck and call when I entered her life as a schoolmate and neighbor, but we hit it off pretty quickly. She was the smartest and most talented girl I had ever met up until that point in my life. We hung out at school and around the block, but we never took our relationship past being buddies until my mom passed away. She was there for me through all the pain and grief. She was such a rock and she single-handily kept me from falling apart and even convinced me to play my senior soccer season even though I was seriously considering not doing it.

We got a lot closer in the months after my mom died, but when she asked me if we could be more, I just froze up. I think I didn't want to risk losing somebody else so important to me again that soon. I hoped that she would have been cool with just hanging out, at least through our senior year and at least until I got my life back together, but she wasn't. We tried to be good friends after that, but she got a boyfriend and we drifted apart.

I immersed myself in soccer and chose to stay home and accept a scholarship to a local university. She couldn't wait to leave town and bailed shortly after graduation for college life on the opposite coast. After that, I heard of how she was doing through Tomislav who proudly updated me on her academic exploits. We saw each other over the holidays and summers from time to time, but it was never the same. She found what she thought was the right person and so did I.

The Gift of Stoppage Time

The memories of our tumultuous past made me smile as I stared down the street. Then that all-too-familiar pain took over my body again and I was shook by the impact of the depth of my newest challenge. It was a challenge that's failure would impact more than just my feelings and would leave a lasting impact on a number of people that I felt very strongly about. I cringed at the thought of screwing the whole thing up and for a minute I admitted to myself that I was crazy for undertaking such a daunting task.

I always felt like I did better when I was alone, but I think it was just my own misconception about my character. Once Chris left the house and I was all by myself again, I did what I had always done best...I stewed. I thought back to how selfish I was when my mom was dying and how I wouldn't stay home on the weekends with her because I didn't want to miss out on a good party instead of staying with her and playing board games and just talking and fully enjoying her company for the last few months of her life.

Failing was something I did a lot of as an adult, but never enjoyed. I didn't want to fail, but I became so used to it that succeeding, no matter how consistent at times, always seemed to be a fluke. I knew that having all kinds of negative feelings wasn't going to help me so I pulled myself together and donned the tuxedo.

It was hideously too big and too bright. I cussed my brother under my breath. I knew he probably had something better at home, but honed in on this one just to add insult to injury. I hoped that his opponents tonight would light him up like a Christmas tree. Hope...at that point, was all that I had.

CHAPTER 12

I dressed quickly and threw up one more time for good measure. I had to get all the nerves out of my stomach before I left the house; otherwise, I figured I'd be throwing up all over town. Then I headed across the street. It was dark and the clock was ticking on everything. As I approached the house I saw a small, orange light on the porch. As I got closer, I realized it was Tomislav smoking a cigarette. Much to my surprise, he looked good. His suit was one of those old-school tweed suits that looked so sophisticated, yet durable all at the same time. He had a hat to match it. Even in the bad light I could tell that he had lost most of the color in his skin, but he still didn't appear to be in too bad of shape for the shape that he was in. He looked much thinner standing up than he did earlier when I had seen him sitting on the back porch. His sturdy build had given way to a much leaner version of Tomislav that I could tell he was none too happy with. As I approached, he took the cigarette out of his mouth and smiled at me.

"Prom was many years ago for you, huh?"

"That's true, but I wanted to look as good as you Tomislav."

"You look good Niko, you look good," he said as he patted me on the back. He started down the steps and I instinctively offered an arm. He stopped cold in his tracks before reaching the first step-down and shot me a familiar look. It was a look that told me not to mess with an old man who could still probably take me apart one-handed. I smiled and nodded him in front of me out of respect. He grabbed my arm and pulled me past him, accepting none of the respect that he interpreted as pity. We started down the street on the four-block walk to Daniel's Field when Tomislav slapped his arm across my chest to stop me only feet into our journey.

"Give me a drink," he demanded.

"You need some water?"

"No, I need good drink...not water."

"I don't understand what you mean."

Tomislav seemed to forget all the physical pain that he was supposed to be in. Instead, he allowed all his anguish and grief to become embroiled in our conversation, of which I was obviously missing the point.

"I need drink Niko. When we go to game we get drink and we enjoy game more. Drink Niko...drink," he said as he made the motion of drinking for emphasis. It was a bad time for my mind to go stupid on me. Fortunately, it finally came around.

"Okay Tomislav, I get it. But should you be drinking in your condition?"

"What do you mean?"

"With all due respect, you're not in the best of health."

Tomislav straightened himself up. He puffed out his chest and sucked in a pretty-deep breath of the crisp, cold, winter air. I was impressed, but worried that he was already expending too much energy too early in the evening.

"What are you talking about? I feel great. Please don't make me get in a bad mood. I have enough people trying to put me in bad mood," he said.

"Like who?"

"Everybody," he declared. I stood next to Tomislav on the sidewalk, only feet from his house, already confronted by the first unforeseen challenge

61

of the evening. I wished that I had somebody to turn to, but Cowboy Chris was busy setting up the field, my brother was rounding up his team, Mr. Nowinski was trying to round up the other team and Angela was storming around town, pissed that she might have entered into the equation too late to do any good.

"There aren't really any places to stop on the way to the field to get something to drink," I said. Suddenly Tomislav picked up his pace to a brisk walk. I started to get worried about all this sudden energy he was exhibiting. I wondered if his night might be predestined to end before I had a chance to even get it started.

"What's the rush?" I asked him as he pulled out in the lead.

"I know a place to get drink," he said as he kept his eyes glued to the sidewalk ahead of him. I followed him down the block and around the corner and up the walkway to a beautiful Victorian House that sat on a huge corner lot. The front yard was covered with overgrown trees and shrubs. It was the type of house that most people would expect to be haunted.

"Who's house--?" I tried to ask before he cut me off.

"Shhh," he ordered.

We reached the huge, wooden porch that extended all the way across the front of the historic house. Tomislav didn't hesitate to approach the front door. I followed cautiously behind him, not knowing where or what he had led me to. Tomislav slowly aimed his shaky finger at the doorbell. The ring was loud enough to wake up plenty of the dead that were buried at the old cemetery just across the street.

The Gift of Stoppage Time

We waited a few awkward moments. I wanted to take off running and leave him all alone, but I knew that wouldn't have been right. A single lock was undone before a gorgeous young blond woman who looked like the bespeckled teacher I fell in love with as a kid, opened the door. Tomislav didn't seem surprised at all by her appearance. He quickly removed his hat.

"Hello...is Goran in?"

"One moment please."

"Thank you."

"Who's house--?" I begged again, only to be cut off once more.

Tomislav put his fingers to his lips to quiet me again. All the mystery was really wearing on me, but I wasn't about to complain. It seemed to be the theme of the whole night. She came back and opened the door all the way and let us in. Then she disappeared down the long, narrow hallway. I looked over at Tomislav. He was gazing up at the beautiful lamps that lit up what was a surprisingly modern house inside. Soft music played through speakers hidden throughout the house. A hint of a smile crossed his face as his breathing labored a bit. I was worried about him, but if it's one thing that the old school guys never let you do; it was to worry about them.

Goran slowly walked down the hall toward us, as his beautiful nurse followed closely behind him. He was a friend of Tomislav's from the old days and was one of the regulars at Daniel's Field every Sunday. Goran didn't play on the championship team with Tomislav, but he did hang out with all the guys. A bout with Polio as a youngster left him too bow-legged to even run properly, but nobody had a passion for the beautiful game, beautiful women and money like Goran did.

He made tons of money buying properties around town back when it was still affordable and then selling it all off when the market got red-hot. He never acquired a taste for settling down with any one woman and even though he never showed up to a game at Daniel's Field with a date, which would have been sacrilege, he was never empty-armed at post-game celebrations either.

He was a tiny, eccentric guy who wore tons of gold jewelry, smoked a pipe and spoke in a voice so raspy that it made you want to reach down into his throat and take out whatever it was that was wreaking havoc on his vocal cords. He greeted Tomislav with a hug and kiss on the cheek.

"Tomislav, it's good to see you. How are you my friend?"

"I'm too skinny. I lost all my muscles, there's nothing left of me."

"You'll gain it all back when you are no longer sick."

"What are you talking about? I'm not sick. I feel good, very good!" Goran seemed to be at a loss for words. So he just stood there and puffed on his pipe as he wondered what Tomislav was doing up and in his house. Tomislav had still been a fixture at his church until the cancer really took hold of him, so many people from around town knew of his battle with the nasty disease. He grew tired of the small talk and leaned into Goran so nobody else could hear them.

"Do you have drink?"

"No, no. She no let drink in the house. I work out now. Get strong, like I used to be before my legs went crooked." He flexed a bicep that revealed nothing. We both laughed and so did he. Goran was always clowning around.

"Why do you need drink?"

"We're on our way to a game."

Goran looked over at me to affirm what seemed to be the outlandish statement. I nodded. Goran might not have known what was going on, but he knew me well enough to know that I wouldn't waste anybody's time and that I wouldn't be walking around town in a white tuxedo unless it was something serious.

"A soccer game?" Tomislav affirmed it with a wink and smile.

"One minute please. I tell her that I leave for a while." Tomislav and I stepped out into the front yard and waited. I noticed that Tomislav was checking out the lights from the stadium that were slicing though the houses across the street. He stood there, mesmerized. He tried to take a deep breath, but an unforgiving cough interrupted its intended entirety. He turned to me, and grabbed my arm tightly.

"On a beautiful night like this, I need drink Niko. We all need drink."

"Can you and Goran get to the stadium on your own?" I asked.

"Niko, we've been doing this a lot longer than you have."

"I'll see you there then," I said as I took off down the street. Then Tomislav turned back towards the brightness that was slicing its way through the houses. He stood there, letting his foggy eyes drink up every bit of the light.

CHAPTER 13

The walk to the liquor store took me into the more gritty part of town. When I was a kid, we used to ride our bikes through this part of town all the time on our way down to the dirt bike track we had built down behind a wherehouse in the harbor. Over the years it became a place that was better steered clear of. But I had no choice. It had to be good drink and it had to be quick. I got some affectionate whistles from some ladies playing cards on an apartment balcony and some odd stares from an older couple on their evening walk.

The front of the small liquor store was full of hoodlums all crowded around the door. I approached with some caution, but felt that I was a little too old to get hassled by what appeared to be a bunch of teenagers with nothing better to do. I got stares of intrigue first and then attitude.

"You're late for the prom bro," said one long-haired, burned-out surfer kid who was missing his front teeth. I ignored the harmless comment and proceeded into the store. The overzealous, overly-paranoid store owner eyeballed my every move as I darted around the store looking for the only drink that would satisfy Tomislav and Goran's tastes. I could have sworn that he had his hand on a gun under the counter, he was acting so jumpy.

After looking through every shelf in the store, I resigned myself to the fact that I was going to have to ask the store owner a question. I approached the counter slowly and without making any unnecessary motions. His body tightened as I moved toward him.

"What do you want?"

I put my hands up to apologize for whatever it was that had him in his mood.

"Do you have Slivovitz?"

He stared at me blankly for a moment and it didn't make me happy. I didn't have time to go anywhere else. I knew I couldn't bring back just any drink either. It had to be Slivovitz. It was a plum brandy that would get rid of your gingivitis just as soon as it would get you silly. Anytime I had somebody tell me that they could actually taste the plums, I knew they were a liar and would always steer clear of them from that moment on. The old-school guys always drank it during the Sunday games. They kept it stored in flasks that they stowed in their jackets. But they would never drink in front of just anybody and they always had enough respect for the kids who showed up at the games to take their swigs in private. The store owner softened his sights on me when he realized that I was actually going to by something from him. He gave me welcome news about the Sliv.

"Yes, I have one bottle left."

"Really?"

"Yes."

"That's awesome!"

He pulled the very recognizable round bottle off the shelf behind him and wrapped it in a plain paper bag for me. He gave me a sinister smile as I left the store like 'good luck getting that where you think you're going.' I took to his non-verbal cue a split-second too late. When I walked out the door into what had become a cold winter night, I was bumped and then robbed by the little punk of a skater. Since he caught me unprepared, it didn't take much to knock me off-balance. I fell into a stack of newspapers, scattering them about, much to the cheers of his buddies who loitered aimlessly. He took off running down the street with what was going to be one of the keys to the evening. I took off running after him as fast as I could as I tried to keep myself from thinking about the Achilles tendon that I blew out years ago. I never fully rehabbed it and never felt totally confident in it ever since then, but was never really forced to test it until now. My middle-aged gallop was no match for his teenage sprint. Fortunately, the streets were pretty empty and I was able to keep an eye on him as he increased the distance between us with every step. He made a quick left turn down an alley I would have chosen not to run down, but I wasn't about to let a disrespectful member of "generation next" get the best of me. I lumbered down the alley after him and wasn't getting any closer to him. In fact, I never would have caught him if it weren't for the trash can he didn't see laying down in his path.

His leg clipped the trash can and it sent him spinning into a garage door and then onto a small stack of pallets. He rolled off the pallets and onto the un-forgiving alley asphalt. The brown bag rolled harmlessly out of his hand and into a shallow gutter that ran the length of the alley. I felt like I was in the air for minutes before I landed on top of his back. Adrenaline was shooting to every limb in my body all at once. I knew I couldn't hit him without going to jail even though he was the one committing the crime. I rolled him over so that I was straddling his chest. I had my fists ready, but decided instead to unleash a few quick slaps to his flushed cheeks.

"Yo man, let go of me," he barked.

"I should kick your butt, you little punk."

I was so pissed that he stole the Slivovitz from me that I wasn't even worried that his friends were on their way to help him out. He seemed to be pretending to be a part of the group in front of the liquor store more than anything anyway.

"Yo, let go of me man!" He barked again to no avail. I grabbed his jacket and shook him around. He tried to throw his hair out of his face so that we could lock eyes and he could try to intimidate me somehow.

"Why should I let go of you? So you can go steal from somebody else?"

"Yo man. I'm dying for a drink man. But I ain't got no dollars," he said. I pulled him to his feet and slammed him against an old, wooden garage door that graffiti artists had fought over to find space on.

"So what if you don't have any cash!" I said. "Then why don't you go get a job?" He just stood there staring at my face as I reamed him up and down about the values of working hard and being honest and not being a complete loser like he obviously was. But the more I yelled at him and tried to make myself feel better, the more I noticed that he had tuned me out and was instead looking at my face with a familiarity I didn't like.

"Hey man. I know you," he said. I stopped shaking him around just long enough to let him continue.

"Yeah right!"

"No, really man. You played in our alumni game a few years ago." I let go of him and stepped back as I tried to remember the last time I was in town for the annual alumni game and also trying to place his face. Hopefully he used to look better than he did now. Because now he had long hair that was neither dread-locked nor curly, it was just ratty. His face had a dirt-tainted tan to it and his body was thin enough to indicate that he didn't have nearly enough calories in the diet he was on.

"What alumni game was that?"

"The Pedro game man," he said with confidence.

"You played soccer at Pedro?"

He shook some dirt off of his tattered sweatshirt and wiped the some sweat and dirt from his face.

"Yeah man. And yo, I was good too. Led the team to playoffs my senior year."

"Playoffs? Big deal. I led them to a State Title," I said arrogantly as I loosened my grip on his sweatshirt. "Are you playing anymore?"

"Nah man. I'm not working or nothing. Just been hanging around, man. I can't even get work down on the docks man."

"How do you live then? Do you just go around stealing from honest citizens?"

"Nah, man. It ain't like that. I work as a mover with my Uncle once in a while, but I gotta get something else brewing man." I could see the desperation in his eyes. I could tell that he wasn't happy to be the loser that he was. He didn't seem to be much older than college age, but it was hard to tell, because it was obvious that his face and body had been taking a beating as of late.

"You ever play college ball?" I asked him.

"Nah...partying got the best of me man."

"Where do you live?"

"Just around, man....wherever. The beach one night...the bleachers at the high school the next...the park, wherever man. Yo, that's my life....whatever and wherever."

"So you're basically homeless?"

"Yeah man! I mean, look at me man. I ain't caught a break in years." There was something about his face that caught my eye. It was that his eyes were different colors. One was brown and one was blue. I did remember who he was after all. He was the kid who was supposed to make it big out of our small town. He was a lightning quick forward who scored goals at will. It was after I left town, but I always got the updates, whether I wanted them or not, from my brother and my brother was saying that this guy was going to make everybody forget what I ever did for the school. It's too bad that the partying got the best of him, because from what I heard, he had more God-given talent that any other player who ever came out of our town. I might not have had the most talent, but I always worked harder than anyone. I wanted to help him for no other reason than I didn't want him to be just another local guy who pissed it all away. The one thing I didn't like was that he smelled like alcohol.

"I can get you a game tonight if you want to test your skills," I said. He sat down on the stack of pallets and motioned for me to give him the brown bag that held the bottle of Slivovitz.

"Yeah, right man. Where?"

"Just up the street. There's a game tonight at Daniel's Field. You remember that place, don't you?"

"I scored some goals there."

71

"Let's see if you still have some if it in you." He leaned back on an elbow as thoughts raced through his mind. He started shaking his head when the reality of what he had become came crashing down upon him. He tugged at his dirty clothes.

"Nah man. Look at me, I look like crap. I can't play like this," he said.

"Nobody at the game will remember what you looked like back in the day. And I can scrounge up some gear for you if you really want to play." He kept shaking his head, just looking down at himself. He pathetically reached out for the brown bag again. I smacked his hand away.

"So are you always drunk?"

"When I can afford to be."

"And now?"

"I'm broke and sober."

"So come play, it'll be good for you. What have you got to lose?" He sat there motionless for minutes as his mind drifted to someplace else. Then he slowly got up off the pallets and shook his arms and legs off. I had no idea what he was going to do next, because he seemed to have drifted into another world. He bobbed his head to an unheard beat, followed by some pretty terrible robotic-looking dance moves. It looked like he was going into convulsions for a moment, though I knew that he wasn't.

"You okay?" I asked him. He stopped it all after a few minutes and suddenly looked like a changed man.

"Yo. That was my goal celebration, man." I didn't want to break his heart, but also felt compelled to be honest with him.

"That's horrible."

"The chicks used to love it."

"Well, I didn't."

"That's because you're not a chick." Then he started bouncing up and down, like a boxer. He was mumbling to himself something that took me a while to figure out. But then it came out cleanly and clearly.

"It's time for me to get my game on man, it's time for me to get my game on," he said to himself between bounces. He moved his feet around the ground quickly, like he was walking dancing on hot coals.

"I still got it man, I'm telling you I do! I know I do man."

"Let's see it then!"

"Yeah, you will man. Everyone will."

CHAPTER 14

I saw the lights in the distance as we headed up the street together. I got a few more intrigued glances from some strangers who passed by us and some snickers from a group of kids playing tag in a front yard. It didn't bother me at all. In fact, the attention felt good. It was the most attention anybody had paid to me in a long time and I was willing to take it, even if they were laughing at me.

"What's up with the tux?"

"It's a long story, I'll tell you later."

"Hey man, what position you gonna be playing tonight?"

"I'm not playing. I've got other things to take care of."

"Who's all playing then man?"

"A couple of local teams, it should be interesting enough." The Kid danced a little more as we approached the stadium. His feet actually moved pretty quickly for a burn-out. I was just wondering if he could blend in with what was going to be the most eclectic mix of soccer players that Daniel's Field had ever seen. And the field had been home to plenty of interesting and dangerous characters for close to a century. I was infamously amongst them.

As we walked in through the chain-link gate and into the cozy, yet well-worn stadium, I could see that Tomislav and Goran were leaning up against the chest-high fence like they always did. The Kid and I walked up the short concrete slope that led us to them. My brother's team was warming up on the field, if you could even call it that. A painfully errant pass almost hit Tomislav in the head and then bounced over us and out the gate and into the street.

My brother's team looked like they were enjoying themselves as they belted errant passes and shots all over the landscape. I cringed whenever I saw one of his teammates prepare to settle a ball, because not one of them ever did that. They all added more touches and more travel to the ball that could have simply been brought to rest on the patchy-grassed field by a more talented player's foot.

"You guys miss me?" I asked smugly as we approached the two old men at the fence. Tomislav and Goran turned around and welcomed me with open arms and bright smiles. Then Goran gave the Kid an unknowing once-over.

"Who is that?"

"Just an old friend I ran into down at the store." Neither of them believed me for a minute, but they were too caught up in the atmosphere to give me grief about anything like a potentially unwanted guest. Besides, Daniel's Field was a place where everybody was welcomed. Back in the day, there would be the old-school guys leaning on the fence and some girlfriends in the bleachers. The referees always sat up on their perch at the clubhouse balcony and Mr. Heinz always took his place up in the press box all by himself announcing the players' names in the worst English imaginable as a collection of people from all around town who paid the couple buck admission fee watched what was some pretty decent soccer from time to time.

I handed the brown bag to Tomislav who took it gently from my hands. He never did take his eyes off of the Kid. From under his jacket Goran produced a beautiful silver flask. They both marveled at the sturdy-looking bottle of Slivovitz. Just the sight of bottle sent shivers down my spine and made me want to dry-heave. The old guys drank the stuff like it was water. Another errant pass flew past our heads. I had seen enough and the game hadn't even started yet. I patted the Kid on the back and headed out through the bent gate that led onto the field. The grass was uneven and a bit too high, just like it had always been.

It also grew in patches and still had a large part of the center of the field that remained dirt from all the use the field got from two local high school football teams that used it. The field was so narrow that your feet hung over the sideline as you sat on the bench waiting for the action to blow by you. I dodged more errant passes and shots as I worked my way over to my brother, who was in goal.

He was dressed like any goalkeeper who had picked this game up late in life and came from a long history of American sports like wrestling and football. He was wearing the sports goggles, the knee pads, the sleeveless concert t-shirt, headband and mouthpiece. And of course, he played without goalkeeper gloves. He refused to wear them and instead did the best he could with his bare hands. I personally think he got the idea when he watched his boyhood idol, Sylvester Stallone play the worst version of a goalkeeper in the classic soccer film Victory. But he would never admit to it.

Watching him and his team warm up was becoming the most painful part of the whole evening, which it shouldn't have been. I finally reached him in goal. His form was non-existent as he blocked shots with his forearms, shins and chest more than with his hands. He seemed unnerved by my appearance next to the goal.

"Hey, could I have a word with you?" I asked him between shots.

"Can it wait? I am in the middle of my warm-up."

"Would it be that much to ask for your guys to try and keep the balls on the field? I mean, we haven't even started playing yet and balls are all over the place."

"Don't say 'your guys' to me...they're your teammates now."

"Whatever. Tomislav may be sick, but his sight isn't that bad yet and he's going to start getting suspicious if it doesn't even resemble soccer." I looked around the field at the misfits that my brother had assembled and who had suddenly become my new teammates. They seemed like nice enough guys, but were unfortunately terrible soccer players. Surprisingly, their inability to perform as soccer players didn't seem to be bothering them at all. Some were laughing and others were walking around the field soaking up some invisible energy from the non-existent crowd as they acted like this was the biggest game of their lives. A few players even kept running back into the locker room to do whatever. I think they were just enjoying having a locker room to go to instead of changing on the sidelines, which was the norm in the local pub leagues.

"Relax, these guys are gamers, not practice players," my brother assured me. I knew he was lying but I didn't have any other options.

"Do you have another team lined up yet?" He asked me as he stepped back into the goal. I looked over at Tomislav and Goran who were happily sharing the contents of the flask with the Kid. The muscles in my stomach started to tighten again.

"They're on their way."
"A.C. Milan?"

"Inter," I said, knowing that my brother didn't know the difference anyway. He was just trying to impress me with something he read on the Internet earlier in the day.

"It looks good."

"What does?"

"The tuxedo," he said. I looked myself over the best I could without a mirror. I was drenched in sweat underneath it all, despite the brisk temperature. Luckily, it didn't show through the white fabric. I walked back towards the fence that surrounded the field when an important detail jumped into my head. I wheeled around and walked back to my brother who was doing pull-ups on the crossbar.

"Do you have another set of uniforms?"

"Maybe...why?"

"I need to let the other team borrow them," I said.

"For the game?"

"No, forever," I said. My brother laughed out loud enough for his teammates to hear. They stopped their warm-ups to listen to the rest of our conversation.

"You want us to just give our away uniforms to the other team?"

"No uniforms...no opponent...no game," I said loud enough so that they could all hear me. My new teammates all shot him cold, hard looks. They would have come unglued if the game had been cancelled at this point. My brother took a look around at his teammates. They all nodded for him to accept the deal.

"Whatever, they're in the locker room. Let's just get this show on the road before all the adrenaline wears off and we start getting tired."

"Thanks."

My brother stepped out of the goal again and this time was blasted by an errant shot in the ear. He grimaced in a pain for a moment, adjusted his goggles then pulled it together long enough to ask me who I had to referee the game. I had bad news for him that he wasn't happy to hear.

"Nobody...yet."

I dropped my head and headed back towards the sideline. I didn't know who I was going to get to referee the game, but I knew that I needed one and I knew that it wasn't going to be me. I looked down at my wrist thinking that I had a watch on, but I didn't, I never did. I guess I was just hoping that something was going to tell or show me that I had more time left than I actually did. I chalked it up to just another in a long line of pipe dreams that constantly took hold of my mind and refused to let go.

I glanced over towards the stadium entrance and out of seemingly nowhere appeared what looked to be close to a dozen teenagers. They were of all sizes, shapes and nationalities. Some were carrying old, beat-up cleats that looked like they had been poached from their dads' closets. Others didn't have cleats at all and sported cut-off jean shorts and tattered shirts. They walked slowly into the stadium and cautiously inspected everything around them. Everyone in the stadium stopped what they were doing to check out one of the last pieces of the puzzle...the other team. Nobody seemed worried too much about the referee situation except me, mostly because nobody except my brother and I knew that there was even such a situation.

I noticed that the Kid had been accepted by Tomislav and Goran and was sharing healthy swigs from the flask with them. I jogged over to them and without warning or apology swiped the flask away from the Kid's mouth mid-swig. He didn't like it at all.

"Hey!"

"You can't be drinking, you're playing...go suit up."

"I can't play man."

"You said you would."

"I changed my mind man."

The guys from the Rec Center casually walked over to the fence and then proceeded to lean against it next to Tomislav and Goran while the Kid and I hashed out our differences. They guys from the Rec Center all sounded very excited. Their voices rose as they all looked around the field at the decently professional set-up we had thrown together in just a few short hours. They made gestures towards the lights, scoreboard and bleachers and laughed out loud at the horrific first-touches of my brother's team. I laid a hand on the Kid's shoulder and guided him away from everybody for a moment. He looked longingly at the flask that I held in my hand like it was a long-lost relative. Without any prompting, Goran started a conversation with the guys from the Rec Center to help make them feel welcome. I tried to keep calm as I put forth my best sales speech to the Kid.

"I need you to play."

"I'm here to party, not play man," he said defiantly, letting the alcohol fuel his courage for the moment. I slowly grabbed his shirt collar again, but thought better of it and let go. I lowered my voice to almost a whisper.

"This game needs somebody who can run with the ball," I said. "You play and then you can party." He reached out for the flask that I held in my hand but I wouldn't let him get to it.

"It's been too long of a time, man. I don't want to embarrass myself."

"The only way you're going to embarrass yourself is by getting drunk out here and not taking advantage of the chance to play again."

"Whatever, I just want to hang out. Is that so wrong?" I took my own healthy swig of the Slivovitz that was stored in the flask. The burning started at my lips and continued on to what felt like my bowels.

"You can hang out your whole life. But a chance like this, to do something special, might never come around again," I said firmly.

"Whatever."

I shoved the flask into his chest and stormed away from him. I was done playing baby-sitter. I walked over to meet the guys from the Rec Center who were being entertained by Goran and one of his many stories. They all seemed excited to have the chance to play, but I saw the disappointment in their faces that my brother's team would be their opponent.

I didn't know how to soften the blow except to tell them that their jerseys were in the locker room waiting for them and that they could keep them after the game in appreciation for their efforts. A few of them gave me high-fives as they headed down the short run of stairs and into the locker room to get ready. An overweight kid with bad acne walked by me with a huge ghetto-blaster radio stuck to his ear. It was cranking out hip-hop nice and loud for everyone within a few square miles to hear. He bobbed his head and smiled at me as he cruised by.

"Game time," he said. I felt empowered for a moment. I felt that the game was actually going to happen. That was, until I saw Tomislav collapse onto the ground just a few feet away from me.

81

CHAPTER 15

By the time I got to him, Tomislav had started to pick himself up. There was no way that Goran could be of much help, since he was half of Tomislav's size. The Kid was too preoccupied with the flask and stared blankly at the field in front of him, probably replaying all the good moments in his life that happened years ago on the same blades of grass. Tomislav slowly rose to his feet and had a puzzled, yet somewhat amused look on his face. He could see the concern on my face, so he quickly extinguished it with a lie.

"I tripped Niko, that's all." The tone of his voice was hardly convincing. He actually let me grab his hand, to help guide him back to the fence that was just a couple of feet away. His perpetually clenched right fist was shut tightly as ever. I felt sick for a moment. I knew that all I could do to make things better was get the game started as soon as possible. All I needed was a referee. Tomislav grabbed the fence tightly and let out a deep breath.

"Maybe the sun will come up before this game starts," he said. I knew that even though he was frustrated that the game hadn't started yet, he was back to his wise-cracking self again. But for how long, nobody, at least nobody walking the face of the earth, knew for sure. And me being worried about it wasn't going to help either.

What I needed was a referee and I had no clue where to find one on a Friday night in the middle of December. Then I felt an arm wrap around my waist that squeezed all the air out of me.

It wasn't the way I preferred to be grabbed. I got ready to try and swing around to hit the perpetrator but caught a glimpse of who it was first before I rained down the hurt on him. It was Cowboy Chris.

"Ya think I left you pardner?"

"No."

"Ya ever thank me for the lights parnder?"

"Not yet. I haven't seen you, where'd you go?"

"Looking for Angela, where else pardner?" I couldn't help but muster a laugh. Cowboy Chris always had an extremely unhealthy infatuation with Angela, but then again, who could blame him?

"Seriously?" I asked, hoping that he had some news to her whereabouts.

"No. I went to round up some of the guys to come watch ya play," he said. I made him let go of me and then led him away from Tomislav, Goran and the Kid. We made our way up the concrete stairs of the clubhouse that sat at the end of the field in the corner above the locker rooms. We both took a seat on an old, wooden bench that sat on the balcony that oversaw the entire field.

"How many times do I have to tell you that I'm not playing."

"Your Achilles thing was ages ago pardner. If you don't mind me sayin' so, I think it's time ya got over it."

"It's not just that, Tomislav is supposed to think that this is a real game."

We watched for a moment as one of my brother's teammates hit a shot that cleared the goal, the old snack bar that sat behind the goal, the twenty-foot high fence that aimed to keep balls in the stadium and then landed in front of a speeding sports car that bumped it down the street the other direction and far out of view. Cowboy Chris raised an eyebrow.

"Ya really think he's gonna to think this is a real game?"

"He's got to," I said defensively.

"Well, I wish ya luck pardner." Cowboy Chris went inside the clubhouse and fired up the scoreboard. He set the clock at forty-five minutes.

"You gotta fix that."

"Fix what?"

"The scoreboard. In soccer, the time counts up, not down." Cowboy Chris fixed it and the scoreboard showed all zeroes.

"Why's that?"

"So the referee can add time to the half for all the stoppages," I said.

"Sounds good to me, let's get this show on the road parnder."

"We're not ready to start yet, I need a ref."

"Well, ya better find one fast pardner, the natives are getting restless." Cowboy Chris pointed me down towards Tomislav, Goran and the Kid who were whistling at the top of their lungs to protest the delayed start. Whistling in soccer was the universal signal of displeasure, and I didn't want these guys expending all their energy before the game even started. Just then I noticed that Tomislav's brother Sasha had pulled up to the gate on his little scooter. I bounded down the steps, skipping every other one in total disregard for my surgically repaired Achilles tendon.

"Where have you been?"

"At ch, ch, church."

"That's cool, did you say a prayer for me too?"

"A, a, actually, I had choir pr, pr, practice."

The Gift of Stoppage Time

I was miffed that Sasha had gone to church to sing instead of pray or that he had even left the whole situation at all. But I respected that everybody had their own way of dealing with these types of situations and the singing must have helped somehow because he didn't look like he had been crying all that much. Even though it was pretty cold out, so much so that we were all breathing a little bit of fog out of our mouths, Sasha was still dressed as I had seen him last, like it was the nicest day of summer. I didn't get it, but it wasn't my job to get it, it was my job to find a referee for the game, and at that point it seemed like Sasha was the only option I had left. Or so I thought.

"Sasha, can I ask you a question?"

"S-s-sure."

"Would you do anything for your brother?"

"A, a, absolutely, y,y, you know that."

"Good, because I need you to referee this game." Sasha looked out onto the field and then over at his brother and the guys at the fence and then back at me. A look of pure terror took over his face.

"I can't d, d, do that."
"Why not?"

"Niko, I can't run and I n, n, never even played the game b, b, before," he said apologetically. I couldn't believe that I was forced to ask him to referee, because I knew he never played, but I was slowly losing it. I was so close to pulling it off and now there was a little thing, like a referee, to keep me from doing it. But I had to have one if I was still going to try and pawn the game off as the real thing to Tomislav.

Even that was stretching it at this point, because even though Tomislav was sick, he wasn't senile. I could tell that it was really bothering Sasha to think that he was letting me down. I put a consoling hand on his cushy, exposed shoulder.

"I was just kidding about refereeing Sasha. I'm glad you made it down here. Is Rose coming over?"

"No, she said the w, w, women never used to come to the games and that she wasn't g, g, going to change that now. She said she w, w, wanted you to call her later though."

"Okay, I will. Did you see Angela today?"

"Yeah, w-w-when I got back to the house after c-c-c-choir to ask Rose where you guys were she was t-t-t-talking to her in the k-k-kitchen."

"How'd she look?"

"Like s-s-she was c-c-crying...a lot." It wasn't what I wanted to hear, but what else was she going to be doing? Her dad was dying and she was coming back to a situation that was worse than the one she left.

"H-h-how's Tomislav doing?" I knew I had to lie, otherwise Sasha might have left at that very moment.

"Good...he was asking about you," Sasha's face lit up and then a tear quickly appeared to roll down his cheek. He wiped it away and then patted me on the shoulder.

"Thanks Niko."

"For what?" He started to choke up and walked away towards the bathrooms. I ran back up the stairs to Cowboy Chris.

He was lying down on the old bench with his cowboy hat over his face, shielding it from the bright stadium lights.

"Get up Chris."

"What's up pardner?"

"I need you to referee this game," Chris sat up and gathered his thoughts. Then he lit a cigarette and looked for a second like he was going to debate me on it.

"If I referee, ya gotta play pardner."

"I can't play. The game is supposed to be real and if I'm out there, Tomislav is going to know that it's not."

"First I get ya the stadium and now I have to referee? What else are ya gonna to ask me for tonight pardner?"

"I'm sure I'll think of something if you give me some time."

"I don't know much about soccer, but I'll try." He stretched out his arms wide and high. I heard multiple bones crack throughout his out-of-shape body.

"You've got to shed the hat though."

"Now...ya know that's not negotiable pardner."

"Fine."

"Do ya have a whistle for me?"

"No."

"I'm sure I can scrounge something up in the clubhouse," he said as the whistles from the guys down below echoed throughout the stadium. I sat down on the wooden bench for a minute. I looked around the small stadium. It was a different view than I was used to having.

The Gift of Stoppage Time

In fact, I don't think I ever sat up on the balcony to watch a game. I knew I couldn't do it tonight either, because I was going to be down with the guys at the fence. It was better anyway, because down along the fence is where all the action happened. I remembered years ago when I used to sneak into games by hopping the fence in the corner of the stadium behind the far bathroom. I always used to stand behind the goal. I could feel the ground shake as the guys stormed down the field at me. I hoped that one day I could play that fast, that hard and that recklessly. It all came true, but the dream didn't last long enough. Not nearly long enough.

The teenagers from the Rec Center made their way onto the field. My brother's team was lined up and ready to go, even though I think that most of them had spent all the energy that they had during their warm-ups. Cowboy Chris made his way to the center of the field, cowboy hat and all. He sported an undersized football (the American version) referee jersey and a pair of those old bike shorts that were way too tight. I couldn't help but laugh at how hideous he looked. But Cowboy Chris didn't care, he never thought about what people cared of him, otherwise he wouldn't have had nearly all the fun he did in his life.

I went to the bathroom and tried to dust off my tuxedo as best I could. I liked the fact that chasing the Kid had worn out the bright sheen of the tux, but wasn't thrilled that I had a less-than-seductive smell to me. I dusted myself off and splashed cold water on my face. I felt pretty good considering the circumstances. I knew that all I could do was take the night one minute at a time, so I tried to relax and do just that. I walked over to guys who were all leaning up against the fence. They were all glad to finally see me standing with them for a moment. Goran handed me the flask.

The Gift of Stoppage Time

I tried to politely reject it, but he wouldn't relent. I took it from him and swigged from the flask again and again. The Slivovitz hit my stomach so hard that it felt like it was burning a hole through my intestines.

I took a deep breath and let the atmosphere of the whole evening engulf me for a moment. The field looked as bad as it always did. The air was cold, but crisp and felt good. The wind was mellow and wasn't whipping up off the water, through the field and up onto the hill like it usually did, which always made playing balls in the air a hectic endeavor.

A few random people from all walks of life started to fill the bleachers. A man in coveralls strolled over from a house across the street and took at seat up in the bleachers with a burger in his grease-stained hand and a bottle of something in a brown bag. A couple of kids from the neighborhood rolled in on their skateboards and took their place up on the clubhouse balcony that had been vacated by Cowboy Chris and I. I looked up at them and waved.

"Do you guys want to do me a huge favor and run the scoreboard?"

"Sure."

I was standing next to Tomislav who had a huge smile on his face. His eyes beamed as he anticipated the opening whistle of a game he could have been waiting years for, for all I knew. For a moment, it didn't seem real, so I shook my head to try and bring myself back to reality. It worked, because then Tomislav coughed mightily into his handkerchief and I could see that part of it had turned red. He tried to hide it by hastily stuffing it back into his jacket pocket, but I saw it. Again, there wasn't much I could do but get the game underway. Cowboy Chris held the whistle to his mouth, but then was interrupted by the kids who were sitting up on the clubhouse balcony.

"The scoreboard just turned off," they proclaimed. We all turned to look up at the far end of the stadium where the scoreboard sat. Sure enough, it was off.

"Turn it back on," I yelled up to them.

"We did," they yelled back in unison. We all looked towards the other end of the stadium again. The scoreboard was not on. I left the guys at the fence and ran up the stairs. I sat with them on the bench for a moment as I tried to figure out how to troubleshoot my umpteenth problem of the night. I noticed Tomislav wave Cowboy Chris over to him. I ran back down to the fence.

"What's going on?"

"He needs a watch for time, I give him a watch," said Tomislav.

CHAPTER 16

When Cowboy Chris finally blew the whistle to start the game a spine-tingling chill rattled my body from head to toe. The game started off very choppy with neither team building any type of rhythm or doing anything that would have made the small crowd rise to their feet. The teenagers chased every loose ball like it was the last one they might ever go after. My brother's team looked out of sorts and wasn't used to playing under the type of defensive pressure that the kids were putting them under. The few attempted passes that my brother's team made went out of bounds. Their first touches sent the ball flying for the heavens. Shots were non-existent, except for one measly attempt that eventually ended up rolling out of bounds for a throw-in.

I had to give the young guys credit though; they did try to dribble past people and actually tried to knock the ball around a little bit. My brother's team preferred instead to just blast the ball downfield and have one of their out-of-shape forwards make a futile attempt at tracking it down though it usually and harmlessly ended up on the foot of their opposition. There were a few brutal clashes in the midfield, but Cowboy Chris kept his whistle out of his mouth and let the soccer resemble the bash-ball of years past. It was something that all of us leaning against the fence could appreciate.

My brother's team ran into the young guys more awkwardly than recklessly, but the kids took exception to it anyway and starting getting in shots of their own. The soccer was limited, but the hits were entertaining enough. I kept trying to catch Tomislav out of the corner of my eye without making it look obvious as the ball would pass by us. He looked mesmerized by the action and I started to think that maybe he had no clue that the game was purely a fabrication. I knew he grew tired very quickly of people pampering him, but I felt compelled to ask him how he felt, even though the ball was still in play.

"Tomislav, are you feeling okay?" He nodded as he brushed me off with an adamant wave of his good hand. Tomislav, Goran, Sasha and the Kid were having a field day with Cowboy Chris every time he made a mess of a thrown-in call. They rained insults in their native tongues on him and Chris would acknowledge them all with a tip of his hat and a smile. Finally, the deadlock was broken when a pencil-thin kid poked home a loose ball from a corner kick. It wasn't beautiful, but it was a goal and we all celebrated it heartily by passing the flask back and forth amongst us a couple of times.

I knew that the quality of soccer certainly wasn't there, but I didn't care. I was just happy we were all at a soccer game and that Tomislav was out of the house enjoying moments that might not ever come again. The Kid apparently didn't have the same view of the game that I did and was making his displeasure known to everybody within earshot of him. I could see that Sasha and Goran were trying to ignore him, but he was getting loud enough that Tomislav had started to take notice a bit too.

I casually walked behind the guys over to the Kid who was getting way out of line with his insults of everybody on the field. He all but could have told Tomislav that the game wasn't real with everything he was screaming out onto the field. I didn't need him ruining everything that I had worked so hard for because he was pissed about his own short-comings as a player and adult.

92

"What are you doing?" The Kid looked at me like I had no business asking him such a question.

"This game is crap man," he said. I put a hand on his back and pulled him in close to me so the guys couldn't hear me.

"Who cares? They're doing the best that they can. This is supposed to be a real game, so quiet down or you're going to ruin it for everybody, namely Tomislav." He shrugged my hand off his back and continued to rain some more insults onto the field.

"Yo...there's no way that anybody is going to mistake that crap on the field for real soccer man," he said. I took a deep breath to try to calm myself, but it didn't work. Fortunately, Goran intervened.

"Is there a problem here?"

"The Kid is just having a hard time keeping his mouth shut."

"About what?"

"About this so-called soccer game," the Kid retorted.

"What's wrong with it?"

"It's horrible man. It's not even soccer. Nobody out there has any skills," asserted the Kid. Goran shook his head and retired himself from the heated debate. I wanted to kick the Kid's butt in front of everyone, but I knew that it wouldn't do any good, because he probably would still have kept talking trash. I decided to call him out it instead, in hopes that his pride would get in the way of him wanting to get more drunk and belligerent.

"Why don't you put your money where your mouth is then and get out there and show everybody what real soccer looks like," I said. He tried to brush me off by laughing about it, but then saw the seriousness in my face.

"They wouldn't know what to do if I stepped out there man. I'd have guys crying," he said with a cocksure grin. Goran stepped back into our argument with a concerned look on his face.

"Won't Tomislav know it's not a real game if he plays?"

"If this poser is willing to step out there to prove to everybody that he still has some game left in him, I'll figure out a way to handle things with Tomislav," I said. I was letting it get personal and I knew that it wasn't a good thing. But I had grown so sick of hearing it from younger guys who were handed everything growing up and never had to prove themselves when it was all on the line. Tonight, it was all truly on the line. I also figured that it couldn't hurt, because in all seriousness, the quality of the game was pretty bad.

"Who you calling a poser man?"

"You! Why don't you go out there and prove it instead of just standing around jabbering about it all night." I have to give the Kid credit for having some guts, because he came after me with his fist clenched and cocked above his head. Sasha easily grabbed it before the Kid could do anything stupid.

"N-n-not right now guys, c-c-come on," pleaded Sasha as he put his mammoth body in between the two of us. I could tell that I had gotten into the Kid's head and I liked it. I was more curious than anyone to see if he could play and my brother's team could have certainly used the help. Both teams could have desperately used the help. The Kid took a long look out at the action on the field. The quality of play was not getting better. It was actually getting worse now that guys were getting tired and there was still a long way to go until halftime. The young guys scored a couple of more goals on breakaways as they took advantage of a defense that had more holes in it than

a slice of Swiss cheese. The Kid grabbed the flask from Goran one last time
and took a healthy swig.

"Yo, I'll play, but I need some gear man."

"Head down into the locker room and grab whatever you need."

"Can I keep it?"

"Keep what?"

"The gear man."

"If you play well you can keep it."

"You don't think I can play, do you?" I wanted him as angry and fired
up as possible when he stepped onto the field. I was also trying to get him to
burn up some of the alcohol he had in his system so that maybe we could
actually see if he had anything to offer the game.

"No...I don't." His face turned red then green as he wheeled around to
vomit onto the walkway.

"Somebody's nervous," exclaimed Goran. Tomislav turned towards us
in time to see him blast chunks to the ground.

He looked amused at the momentary sideshow, but quickly turned his
attention back to the game which had unfortunately degenerated into a
glorified game of kick ball. Goran offered to take the Kid down to the locker
rooms to get cleaned up and into uniform. I knew that I had to preface what
was going to happen next to Tomislav somehow. He looked like he was
having such a good time.

His eyes never left the flight of the ball. A perpetual, half-cocked grin
had occupied his face since the game kicked off. He and Goran traded a
running commentary on the game and shared laughs during stoppages in play.
I approached Tomislav cautiously, not wanting to distract him from the game.

I touched his arm lightly to get his attention. He turned to me and looked annoyed by my interruption.

"Tomislav, could I talk to you for a minute?"

"At halftime please, not during game Niko."

"But it's kind of important." Tomislav politely took the flask from Sasha's hand and extended it towards me.

"You need drink Niko, you too nervous." The words started to come out of my mouth, but I didn't want them to. I had no idea what the repercussions would be, but I felt compelled to be honest with him. Especially after all we had been through in our lives. I started to mutter something that got his attention off the field and onto me and then the words just came out.

"Tomislav, I need to be honest with you...this isn't a real--." Tomislav put a hand up to my face and brought the most important confession of my life to an unceremonious end. Then he lowered his hand and directed his attention back to the field. I didn't want to stop. I wanted to tell him. I had to tell him, because otherwise I wouldn't be able to live with myself for not being honest with him. I ignored his previous wish and valiantly tried to come clean with him again. I blurted it out awkwardly and wished that I could have taken it back the second it left my lips, but it was too late.

"This isn't a real game." He never looked at me. He just kept watching the action unfold in front of him with the same half-cocked grin that he had been wearing on his face since the minute he walked into the stadium. The ball went out of bounds and Cowboy Chris stopped the game for a minute so that an injured player could be tended to. Tomislav then dropped his head and starting shaking it ever-so-slightly.

I wanted a do-over worse than I ever had in my entire life. I wanted an out. I needed an out. But I wasn't going to get one.

"It is a real game Niko. It's always a real game," he said without a trace of disappointment in his voice. He turned to me, took a look at my ghost-white face and smacked it affectionately. I smiled at him and tried to hide a tear that crept down my cheek. He pretended not to see it and directed his attention back to the field.

CHAPTER 17

The smell of the locker room hadn't changed since I had last been in it, which was years ago. But then again, why would it? The flooring was still the same old, small, light blue and off-white hexagonal tiles that held a history of odor that would knock anybody with any sense of smell completely on their butt the minute they opened the door. It was a wonder that my feet didn't completely fall off after so many years of not wearing anything on my feet before and after games. The mirror where you could check yourself out in on your way out to the field still hung by the door, but way too low for anyone more than five feet tall. The cages in the back of the locker room that used to hold all our duffle bags and extra uniforms were still locked and held a bunch of random pieces of football (the American version) equipment and some free weights that looked like they were used in ancient times. But it was all apropos, because the gritty setting in the locker room exemplified everything that soccer at Daniel's Field was about; all guts and no glory.

I couldn't help but think back to the times that I was thrown out of games for too many ill-timed tackles and would storm into the locker room looking for something to throw or break. The problem with breaking anything was that they would charge you for it and looking for something to throw was usually an act in futility since everything during games was usually locked up in the cages anyhow. I did take joy in throwing the big, plastic trash can around the room while cussing the referee until I ran out of breath.

It usually resulted in me spending my post-tirade minutes cleaning everything up before my teammates returned to the locker room after grinding out what was hopefully a good result.

The dingy and cramped visitor's locker room had a festive mood to it since the young guys were owners of what seemed like an insurmountable 3-0 lead, especially since most my brother's team had to almost be carried off the field at halftime. Hip-hop music blared from the oversized radio that sat in the corner on a table that looked more suited for a medieval torture chamber than for a pre-game massage. I surveyed the entire group of young guys quickly from the doorway. They all looked like they were having a great time. They danced and lip-synced to the music on the radio. Most of them had probably never even been in a locker room before, so they were taking it all in. One kid even came out of the shower with a big smile on his face as his teammates all razzed him for taking a shower at halftime.

But I guess he figured that when something doesn't happen very often, like playing under the lights in a stadium with locker rooms and showers that he might as well enjoy it to the tilt. I agreed wholeheartedly with him. As I scanned the room, a big problem became evident to me, there were only ten guys. I counted again, and tried to keep track of them accurately as they all seemed to be bouncing in all different directions, enjoying every single moment of their big-time halftime. I wasn't off in my count; there were only ten players in the locker room. I was sure that they played the first half with a full side, but I had to ask just to confirm that I wasn't crazy.

"You guys missing somebody?" I yelled out to nobody in particular. Out of respect for me, the little guy with acne quickly rushed over the turned the music down a bit. I repeated myself.

"You guys had eleven players, didn't you?" One of the better players on the team, a well-muscled player who had tattoos covering his entire shaved head, rose to his feet.

"He had to go to work," he said. It wasn't something that I wanted to hear because I was going to have the Kid play for my brother's team, whether he liked it or not, because they were the ones that desperately needed the infusion of youth obviously more than the young guys.

"You got anyone we can use?"

"Give me a minute, I'll see what I can do," I said.

I popped out of the locker room and noticed that my brother's team hadn't yet gone into their locker room. They all loitered around aimlessly, their bright-red faces searching for energy reserves they probably didn't have stored in their bodies.

"What's up?"

"Door's locked."

"Shouldn't be."

"Well, it is. Because we are certainly not standing out here in this cold for our health," he barked back at me. I tried the door and it was locked. Since I didn't see the Kid, I figured it was his doing. I knocked. Nobody replied. I knocked harder the second time and yelled for him.

"Hey Kid, you in there?" I

"Yeah...and it's DJ!"

"What?"

"My name man...it's DJ!" My brother's team grew restless as they milled around the door. The grumbling amongst them grew louder and louder with every passing moment as if the delay was the sole reason for their inability to play the game at any sort of competent level.

"You'll get a name when you do something special. So, are you going to open up or what? There's a whole team out here waiting to get inside."

"No way man! I ain't opening the door for nobody. These shorts are hideous," he said. I didn't know what he was talking about and had reached my limit of playing games for the evening.

"You've got to open the door Kid. I'm sure we can sort it out somehow." A few moments passed and then I head the door get unlocked. I opened it slowly, and started to go inside with my brother's entire team following closely behind. The Kid was standing in the middle of the locker room with a pair of shorts that were more suited for a seven-year-old than an average-sized adult. Everybody in the room tried the best they could for a few minutes to hold back, but then the laughter erupted out of everybody. The Kid angrily tried to peel off the shorts in frustration as some of the guys in the room had to fight themselves to hold back tears.

"Shut up guys," I begged. "He's going to be helping you out in the second half." The Kid stopped trying to remove his shorts momentarily.

"I ain't playing with these guys man. Screw that!"

"Way to go," I whispered to my brother who was right next to me. He burst out laughing again, as did his whole team. The shorts were bad, they could have almost been described as a glorified Speedo, but I would have kept my feelings to myself if I were them, at least until after the game and until after the Kid scored some goals for them.

"No way am I playing for these guys," reiterated the Kid. Everybody stood there inspecting his appearance. I was wondering whose shorts he even got and who on the team would have had shorts that small anyway. I wanted to laugh too, but held back because I knew that if the Kid left, it would just make my life more difficult.

"Those are my wife's running shorts," confessed Dave. He was a nerdy, computer science teacher that was easily the worst player on the field in the first half.

"She must have thrown them in there as a joke when I left for the game tonight, because I bailed on our weekly Scrabble game to come here," he said. Everybody erupted in laughter again and the Kid's face got redder with anger. He tried to storm out of the locker room, but I stopped him. He continued to try and push me, which pissed me off, but I slowed him down and guided him out of the locker room and out towards the string of water fountains that separated the two locker rooms from each other.

The young guys had gathered outside of their locker room to see what all the fuss was about. My brother's team came to their senses and poured out onto the area between the two locker rooms that was nothing more than a narrow, cracked-concrete path and a small hideously uneven grass area that we used to use to warm up on before games. The Kid and I argued about whether he was going to play with my brother's team when we were interrupted by Xavier, the shaved-head player for the young guys.

"How about him?" He asked me while pointing at the Kid. I was surprised that they even wanted him, especially considering that he still had the hideous shorts on.

"I was going to have him play with the older guys," I said.

"Yeah, but we need the player." My brother and his teammates were grumbling amongst each other loudly as they, realized they might have angered the only chance that they had to get back into the game.

"There's no way you can let them pick up the Kid," said my brother angrily as he entered the negotiation at the prompting of his teammates.

"We need a player...and it's got to be him...otherwise we're taking off," demanded Xavier. Both teams were out of their locker rooms and were pretty much squared-off in between the two locker rooms. Tomislav, Goran, Sasha and even Cowboy Chris had all taken position at the top of the short run of stairs that led the players off the field and down into the locker rooms. Nobody seemed to know what was going to happen next. But in the old days when teams squared off like that, it always resulted in a fight. I think that whoever built the locker rooms so close together did it for that sole reason, to put the teams close enough to each other so that when they did decide to fight, they didn't have far to travel.

I tried to get my mind working to figure out a quick and easy solution to what was quickly becoming a big mess, but my mind was going numb on me and I was starting to get very tired from what had become a very long day.

"The Kid should play for the old guys. They're behind and need the help," I announced to everyone in my best authoritative tone. The young guys let out a collective groan and shot me cold stares. My brother's team gave each other high-fives and started to celebrate like they had just won the game and failed to realize that all they might have been picking up was a burned-out kid in an undersized pair of shorts that everybody thought could play some soccer.

"I ain't playing for those guys man. And I ain't gonna tell you again," insisted the Kid. "Then we'll take him," said Xavier. The Kid waved-off my brother's team and strolled over to the young guys who welcomed him with open arms and then disappeared with him back into their hip-hop themed locker room.

"Good job guys, you just scared off the only chance you had at getting back into this game," I said. They all argued amongst each other for a few minutes while I took a long drink out of the old water fountains. The water tasted as warm and stale as it always had. I rose up from my drink and was met with dozens of curious stares.

"We do have one other chance to get back into this game," said my brother as he approached me to lay a hand on my shoulder.

"If you play with us, we have a chance to win this thing," he said. I heard a laugh erupt from the guys who were standing at the top of the steps. I looked up at them and they all pumped their fists at me, encouraging me to do it.

Tomislav stood up there with his arms crossed and gave me a little nod. There was no way I could say no at that point. No matter how worried I was about embarrassing myself. I hadn't played a real soccer game in a few years. I blew out my Achilles tendon and then just lost interest in coming back to what was just a bunch of hacker-infested Sunday League games played in front of nobody on rock-hard park fields. I messed around with the ball from time to time with some kids in the neighborhood and even did a little bit of coaching, but nothing that compared to playing in a real game.

My first concern wasn't how well I could play; it was if I could play at all. But running after the Kid had proved to me that my Achilles could hold up if it had to; I was only worried about how much gas I had left in the tank after chasing the Kid for what felt like many miles.

"Let's do it then," I said confidently as I threw all caution to the wind.

My new teammates excitedly patted me on the back as the little bit of food I had left in my stomach started creeping up my throat. I took a deep breath and looked up the stairs at Tomislav and the guys. They yelled encouragement at me, but it just made me more nervous. I have to admit that it did feel good to hear though, after years of living in the anonymity of adulthood and not having been recognized for doing anything special with my life since the last time I set foot on the same field.

"Let's get you a uniform," said my brother. My brother had stashed his own field uniform deep in his duffle bag so that the young guys couldn't get to it. The rest of the team left the locker room and headed out into the cold night for the second half. I sat by myself on the worn wooden bench and put on my borrowed uniform. It fit well and felt good.

My brother had even left me a pair of extra shin-guards. They were the kind of shin-guards that had ankle guards and covered most of your lower leg. There was no way I was going to wear them. In fact, the last time I played at Daniel's Field was way before any leagues were making them mandatory and I always wore my socks rolled down around my ankles which left my shins dangerously exposed to some brutal hits. But it was me that was always doing the hitting, so all I had to fear was my own reckless abandon.

I wasn't in the mood to get overly cautious about my own well-being so I hurled the shin-guards into the shower area and proceeded to put on a borrowed pair of cleats. It always took me five or six tries to get my left foot to feel just right in my left cleat and tonight was no different. I put the left cleat on, then took it off, then adjusted my sock and then repeated the whole process over again six times. It finally felt pretty good. I rose to my feet and tucked in my shirt, and then un-tucked the back. Despite the cold temperatures outside, I went over to the sink and ran water through my hands and then ran my hands through my hair. I squatted down to inspect my appearance in the mirror that was too low. I didn't look half bad. I thought about stretching in the locker room, but figured it would be better to get out on the field and start soaking up the atmosphere as soon as possible.

Back when I played at Daniel's Field in my late teens and early twenties, I didn't think anything of it. I showed up for games in ratty t-shirts, surf shorts and sandals and left games in the same manner. I used to scoff at the older guys on my team that showed up in fancy shirts and slacks and dress shoes. I used to wonder why they were making such a big deal out of what I viewed as simply a stepping stone to a more brilliant career.

For me, unfortunately, it ended up being the pinnacle of my career and not merely a stepping stone. I wished that I had enjoyed the moments back then as much as the older guys on my team did. I took one last look around the empty locker room before I went out onto the field and promised myself that this time around I was going to enjoy it. Suddenly, it all felt the same as it did years ago.

All the smells were familiar. Many of the sights were the same with the exception of a few subtle changes. I didn't feel sick to my stomach, I felt good. I slowly walked out of the locker room and up the steps out onto the field.

CHAPTER 18

Tomislav and the guys were pressed up against the chest-high chain link fence where I entered the field. I noticed that Mr. Nowinski had made it over from the Rec Center, which was something special, because he never left that place. I heard the other locker room door slam shut and turned to see the Kid coming out onto the field. He had his socks pulled up over his knees, and his shin-guards in place. He had his shirt tucked in nice and neat and had even found a shoe-lace to tie his hair with like all the young pros were doing. He was the kind of player that never made it more than a few games back in the day, because the Greater Los Angeles League wasn't a good stage for those kinds of dancers.

"Let's see what you have in your little bag of tricks," said Goran.

"Watch and learn old man," the Kid shot back arrogantly at him. Tomislav reached out and grabbed him by the sleeve.

"You know what the fence is for?"

"Yeah old man. It's to keep the fans off the field."

"No, no, no. It's to keep the players on it." All the guys laughed as they left the Kid to figure out what it meant all by himself. The Kid yanked his shirtsleeve from Tomislav's grasp and swaggered out onto the middle of the field. I started to walk out towards the middle of the field when I heard Tomislav call out to me.

"Come here Niko, please." I walked over to him slowly and hoped that he wasn't maddened by the fact that he knew that it wasn't a so-called official game. He laid a strong hand on my shoulder as Goran and Sasha leaned in so that they could hear what Tomislav had to say.

"You have to hit him," he said. I smiled, but Tomislav stayed very serious. "He has no respect for the game and his voice is making my head crazy."

"I will, for sure Tomislav." He pulled me in close to him and whispered to me.

"Hit him so hard that he will feel it for the rest of his life," he said solemnly. I pulled back from Tomislav and took a long look at him. He was as serious as he ever was. I knew Tomislav didn't want me to punch or elbow him, what he wanted was the kind of slide tackle that even the people in the bleachers could feel the impact of. The Kid had obviously set him off and now Tomislav was making it my job to send the message that you can't just stroll into Daniel's Field and start talking trash. The right to talk trash had been earned with blood and sweat by players for over a century and Tomislav wasn't about to let that change tonight. He smiled and then let out a ferocious cough. Cowboy Chris bounded down the stairs of the bleachers to start the second half after hanging out with some guys from work who had showed up and were giving me flack for how tight my jersey fit across my midsection. He got out to the center circle and gave a quick, short whistle to indicate that it was time to start the second half. I jogged out to him and could already feel my muscles tightening up. He met me with a curious smile.

109

"I reckon this night just got a whole lot more interesting."

"Easy with that whistle okay? Because the Kid and I are going to be going at it all night," I assured him.

"I don't give a crap about that pardner...Angela just got here." I stood frozen for a moment in the middle of the field, unable to turn my direction back towards the clubhouse where she stood. Cowboy Chris had his gazed fixed that way and wasn't about to break it, not even for the start of the second half.

"You serious?"

"I wouldn't mess with ya about something like that pardner." I slowly turned around to see her at the fence with the guys. Goran and Sasha took turns giving her huge hugs and kisses while Tomislav kept his back turned to her and his attention fixed to the field. I couldn't tell if Tomislav even knew that she was there and was intentionally blowing her off or if he was so fixated on the action at hand that his concentration wouldn't allow him to realize that his long-lost daughter was only inches behind him. Cowboy Chris raised the whistle to his mouth, but then lowered it when he realized that I wasn't taking my eyes off of the action that was unfolding over in the corner of the field.

I saw Angela slowly let go of her Uncle Sasha and then lean on the fence next to her dad. They stood there leaning on the fence next to each other for what seemed like hours. Then Tomislav, without even looking over at her, raised his arm and gently placed it around her. She leaned her head against his body as he pulled her in tightly to him, all the while never taking his eyes off the field.

Nobody seemed to realize the impact of the moment expect me and maybe Chris.

Everybody else fidgeted around while they patiently waited for the beginning of the second half. I let out a sigh of relief, because even though I couldn't imagine Tomislav ignoring his only child on a night like tonight, I also knew that he was incredibly hurt when Angela left town for what she thought was the man of her dreams.

It was hard to admit, but the Kid actually looked like he could play even though he was decked-out like the posers I used to love to hit with crunching tackles anytime I could get close enough to them. He did have the "look" of a guy who could pose problems if you gave him too much room to operate. He had long, lean legs that still looked like they had some soccer muscles in them. As I watched him gallop around the field warming up, I could tell that his long strides were not going to be much fun to catch up to. But the beauty of Daniel's Field was that the field was so tight and cramped that no matter how well they tried to hide, I would always find them sooner or later.

My brother's team seemed to have a new sense of confidence to them and I hoped that it wasn't all due to the fact that I was on the field, because that would have only added to the already over-whelming amount of pressure that I felt. They started calling out to each other, telling each other to be ready to rock and roll and all kinds of crazy talk. I should have told them to keep quiet about it until I actually did something to warrant their over-confidence in me.

111

The Kid couldn't stand still as he waited at midfield with his striking partner ready to get the second half underway. I sat in behind the forwards, deep in the middle of the field like I always had. I didn't care about being out wide on the flanks where the grass was nicer and the crowd was closer, the real players all loved to grind around in the middle of the field where so much of the thankless, yet critical work was done. I felt my heart beating quicker and the thought crossed my mind that I could possibly have stolen Tomislav's thunder by having a heart attack right there on the field before the second half had even started. I took a quick look over towards Angela before the whistle sounded, but before her and I could even make eye contact, I was unceremoniously interrupted by the sound of the Kid's voice.

"Looks like it's the old guard verse the new school."

"You do have life insurance, don't you Kid?"

"That's funny old man. Just don't get too pissed when I spin you into the ground."

"Do what? Spin who? That's a lot of smack coming out of the mouth of a guy who could never keep it together long enough to do any of those things past high school." It was a cheap shot and I meant it to be, somebody had to humble the Kid a little bit. He started shaking his head emphatically and chewing on his lip. I could tell that he wanted a piece of me and he was going to have that chance in a matter of seconds if I didn't get a chunk of him first.

Cowboy Chris blew the whistle and the Kid got the ball off of his teammate and immediately tried to go solo through my whole team. He blew past our forwards without too much effort, but then was faced with having to get by me. I moved towards him with short, choppy steps and tried to make sure that I had my body positioned properly. As he got closer, he wound up his leg like he was going to clip the ball out wide. I extended my leg to try and block it and unfortunately for me, he faked the pass and tapped the ball through my legs. I couldn't believe that the Kid had nut-megged me in the opening seconds of the second half!

The small, but vocal crowd let out a pretty loud roar at my expense. The Kid then beat another midfielder and cracked a shot that my brother had no chance to get to. Luckily, it kept rising and sailed harmlessly over the crossbar. I couldn't believe I let him do that to me, and cussed myself as I positioned myself for the ensuing goal kick. Instead of running back to his spot, the Kid took the extra effort of tracking me down.

"It's gonna be a long half for you if that's the best defense you got man," he said. I couldn't believe the Kid had the guts to talk so much trash. After all, I was the one who got him the game in the first place. The guys on the fence and Angela gave me a bad time for getting megged and continued to egg me on to get a good hit on the Kid.

"S-s-shut the K-k-Kid up for g-g-good," yelled Sasha. Tomislav just leaned in silence against the fence with his arm draped firmly around his beautiful daughter. I looked over in time to see Angela take an incredibly healthy swig from the flask. I also noticed that the crowd had filled up with a few more random people and that a handful of guys from the Rec Center had come over and taken their place at the top of the bleachers.

They rained down good-natured insults on their friends on the young guys for playing too slowly and for misdirected passes. I wanted the ball, but also wanted a chance to light up the Kid. I knew I couldn't focus on both at the same time, so I worked to get the ball at my feet, because there was also a three-goal deficit to be made up.

My legs throbbed unmercifully and felt like they were filled with lead weights after just a few short sprints. I hoped that I would get my second wind quickly, because even though we were playing a full forty-five minute long half, I knew that it would fly by the same way that the entire evening felt like it was going. I finally got a ball at my feet in the midfield and turned, thinking I had some time to do so. I was met with a crunching knee-high tackle from none other than the Kid. I didn't expect it and was hit awkwardly. I went sprawling to the ground. I heard a loud whistle just a second later. The Kid made his displeasure with the call known to Cowboy Chris who had run over to see if I was okay.

"You gonna bail your friend out all night man?"

"Relax pardner...just play the ball from now on."

"Guy's gotta try to stay on his feet ref."

"Play the ball, or you'll be outta here," warned Cowboy Chris. I felt weak and stupid for letting him get such a good shot on me. But nobody on my brother's team knew enough to tell me that I had a man on me and it was really just all my fault for not having the vision to see that he was coming in on me. The game continued its choppy ways with nobody except the Kid and me trying to settle the ball when we had the chance.

My brother's team, or should I say, my new team, continued to labor as the game got older and their passes rarely hit their intended target. I was trying to get my heavy legs to certain points on the field to break up plays, but I was always a second or two late. The Kid kept getting the ball in good spots on the field and cracked a couple of more shots that forced my brother to make some pretty good saves. The Kid's trash-talk was incessant.

"Hey man, you carrying a refrigerator on your back or what?" The Kid's confidence was filling up with each good touch and each solid shot. I was getting more and more tired of chasing people around the midfield. My brother even started barking at me to get back quicker and to talk more. I was trying to do everything I could to keep from passing out, because I was gassed. I was also sick of everybody expecting me to help them out. I wondered if anybody was ever going to help me out.

Luckily enough, the play got muddled around the midfield and I finally pounced on a loose ball. I gobbled it up after throwing a couple of forearms and dribbled away with it. Then I played a crisp pass out wide to my right midfielder and kept my run going towards their goal. I hoped that he would have played a ball to my feet, but he decided to try and lead me through with a long ball that I didn't have a chance in hell of tracking down. I gave it a half-hearted effort and then stopped my run when it felt like my heart really was going to explode through my chest. I bent over and tried to catch my breath. I heard the whistle sound as Cowboy Chris had their goalie kick the ball out of bounds so I could catch my breath. Cowboy Chris made his way over to me.

"You okay pardner?"

"Not sure," I said. I put my hands on top of my head like coaches had told me over the years to do when I was short of breath. I didn't care how long the stoppage was, so I slowly made my way down the sideline and over to the fence where the guys and Angela were standing and leaned against it.

I must have looked terrible, because nobody said anything, they just stared at me. Goran extended the flask towards me, but Tomislav made him put it back. I took a few deep breaths hoping to fill my lungs with much-needed oxygen. The air was cold and crisp and smelled like the Holidays. A light fog had rolled in off the harbor and the wind had kicked up. Everyone except Angela looked worried about me. Our eyes met and she smiled and then sort of laughed at my pathetically out-of-shape state.

"You're back."

"For now," she said coyly. I wanted to stand there and talk to her all night and find out what she had been up to all those years that I didn't see her. But I knew it wasn't the place or the time. Tomislav grabbed my jersey.

"You have to get the Kid with a good tackle Niko. Do you hear how much he's talking out there?"

"Yeah I can hear it. I'm closer to him than you are," I shot back out of frustration. Tomislav didn't take it personally and could tell that I was laboring. I looked over at Angela who was still smiling. She had seen my temper plenty of times before and could tell better than anyone that an explosion of it wasn't too far away. I still heard the Kid chattering away behind me to anyone within earshot. The way he was talking, you would have thought that Manchester United had a helicopter on the way to pluck him right off the field and into their starting lineup.

He was doing some good things, but against garbage competition and I was having a hard time getting anything going, which was really taking its toll on me physically, mentally, but mostly emotionally. He was all over Cowboy Chris to get the game going again. I looked at Tomislav, who looked a little tired.

116

"How you feeling?" I asked him, trying not to sound too motherly.

"Not bad...how are you?"

"Tired. The Kid is running me ragged."

"Then you must do something about it." He took his arm off of Angela and extended his hands out in front of me. Then he made the motion with both hands like he was breaking a stick into two. I knew exactly what he meant and so did everyone else. It was obvious to me that the score of the game didn't matter to them as much as it did that I got a good shot in on the Kid. But I still wanted to win the game, because I knew that if I lit the Kid up but let him beat me, I would never hear the end of it, no matter how gruesome of a tackle I hit him with. I tried to summon up any energy that was hiding in my body somewhere, but it didn't seem to be working. Cowboy Chris blew his whistle to get the game going again. I readied myself for more action and let go of the fence. I turned to run back onto the field when Tomislav called for me.

"It's good to see you play again Niko," is all he said as he wrapped his arm back around his shivering daughter. I felt a surge of energy explode through my body. I asked Cowboy Chris how much time there was left in the second half. He took a long look at the watch that Tomislav had given him to help him keep time when the scoreboard went on the fritz.

"Twenty minutes."

"Don't forget stoppage time," I reminded him sternly. He nodded in agreement and I realized that stoppage time was probably going to get stretched as long as was needed. It was little comfort considering that we were still down a sizeable three goals. I ran back onto the field and the Kid made a point of going out of his way to try and bump me. I avoided him by straight-arming him.

"Hey man...did you tell her that you love her?"

"It's none of your business punk."

"You should focus on getting goals instead of getting dates."

"You should make sure to hop every time you get rid of the ball," I said alluding to the fact that I intended on coming in on him high and hard with a tackle every time that he played a ball. My first touch after the brief stoppage was a good one and I launched a driven-ball deep into the corner of the field for one of our fairly capable forwards. He collected it and lucked out when his defender slipped. He touched the ball past another flat-footed defender and slotted home our first goal of the game. We were only two goals down but had no subs. Guys were getting really tired and we were having a hard time linking up the most simple of passes. The young guys were still playing and were mostly relying on getting the ball to the Kid who then put his head down and tried to beat our entire team en route to the goal. I got close enough a couple of times to bump him off the ball ever-so-slightly so that my teammates had enough time to come in and double-team him and put an end to his forays into our end of the field.

After a few minutes of choppy play that hardly saw the ball stay in bounds for more than seconds, the Kid tried to turn a ball out of his own end. I stuffed him good. The ball popped loose to another one of my forwards who actually sent a pretty nice lofted shot over the helplessly out-of-position goalie's head.

We were within a goal with about ten minutes left. The Kid was pissed. He took the ball right off the kickoff and tried to juke through all of us again. I went in on him and tried to bump him off the ball but he got an elbow up and popped me in the mouth with it. He drew blood instantly and I fell to the ground. Cowboy Chris ran over and stepped in between us, because he knew that I was going to go after the Kid for his cheap shot after I got up. I sprung to my feet and tried to juke my way around Cowboy Chris. He pleaded with me to resist launching a payback assault on the Kid. I complied with his request because he was a friend and I knew that I would have another shot during the run of play to tattoo the Kid eventually. Since Cowboy Chris didn't have any cards, he issued a verbal warning to the Kid that his next infraction would result in expulsion.

"This is street ball man, there ain't no cards in street ball," he said defiantly to Cowboy Chris. At that moment, he gave up his right to finish the game in one piece. I took a look over at the guys and Angela at the fence. They all urged me on with pumps of their fists and by mimicking breaking somebody in two. Goran even made the gesture of slicing his throat, which might have been a tad excessive. But it was vintage Daniel's Field and I loved it. The next time the Kid got the ball he tried to spin me as I clipped at his heels from behind. He started to get around me and then I lifted my leg higher and dumped him in the middle of the field in the moist dirt.

"You dirty--," he said before Cowboy Chris interrupted him.

"You got the call Kid, relax," lectured Cowboy Chris. His team set up for a free kick just inside of their half.

While the Kid took his time dusting himself off in order to try and run more time off the clock, I went around to my teammates and told them to hold our defensive line just inside of midfield.

"But the ref said he wasn't going to call offside," said Dave the nerd. I told him not to worry about it and guaranteed him that if we all held our line that the referee would surely give us what would be the easiest of obvious offside calls. They all shook their heads but promised me that they would comply with my odd tactical request. I ran up to Cowboy Chris and nudged him.

"Don't call it, okay?"

"Call what?"

"The obvious offsides you're going to see here," I said. I wasn't even sure that he knew what offsides was, but I knew that even though my team wasn't going to plead for the call, people in the crowd probably were.

"Okay...whatever you want pardner," he said. I wished for a moment that dealing with referees my whole career had been that easy and painless. Xavier lined up his free kick and drove it deep into the corner, where the guys and Angela were standing. My entire team held their line like I had asked them to and raised their hands in unison as they appealed for an offsides call. Cowboy Chris held his whistle. It was just the Kid and I who gave chase to the ball.

"See ya," the Kid yelled at me as he left me in the dust for a moment and took off for the ball. I tried to hold him before he took off, but missed when I tried to grab a handful of his jersey. All I had to do was track him down in the corner and get a hit on him before he got out of it.

120

The Gift of Stoppage Time

I wheeled around about as fast as a cruise ship could turn and started pumping my arms and legs. He had quite a few steps on me, but it didn't matter because he still had to get to the ball, control it and then head for the goal. All I had to do was get to him before he could get out of the corner. I could hear Angela and the guys pleading with me to catch him. I didn't even think about my Achilles tendon as I launched into the longest sprint I had made in ten years. Every step I made begged to rip a muscle or tear a ligament, but my body held up its end of the bargain. The Kid got to the ball in the corner well before I did. But then he made a fatal mistake. Instead of simply taking a couple of touches to turn the ball, he decided to do a fancy spin turn. It was easily the worst decision of his young adult life.

As he went to spin, his foot caught on the top of the ball and he fell. He looked up to see me barreling down on him like a freight train. He quickly scrambled to his feet. The ball had squirted away from him and was rolling out of bounds right in front of Tomislav and my personal cheering gallery. The Kid caught up to the ball, turned and tried to push it past my incoming tackle. His feeble attempts to get out of my way came way too late. As I got closer to him, it all went silent. I couldn't hear anything. I launched into my tackle and was in the air for what seemed like minutes. Since he never played in the Greater Los Angeles Soccer League, the Kid had no clue how high you had to jump to avoid a tackle.

I hit him so hard that it rattled my insides. He went flying not just into the fence, but over it. The guys tried to catch him, but he got blasted right through them. I lay on the ground for a moment and wondered if I had done myself as hard as I had done him. Cowboy Chris charged over, whistling frantically.

121

The Kid jumped back over the fence and onto the field and came running at me with his fist clenched above his head. I had to admire him for surviving the tackle in the first place and also for having the guts to come after me after such a tackle.

He got close enough to swing at me, but too far away to hit me. He ended up connecting with the back of Cowboy Chris' head. The blow sent Cowboy Chris into a profanity-laced tirade. Everybody in the small crowd was on their feet. My brother ran over to help intervene and he kept the Kid away from me, which was for the Kid's own good anyway.

"That's got to be a red card man," demanded the Kid.

"I thought you said this was street ball," countered Cowboy Chris.

"He didn't even come close to getting the ball man, that guy can't play."

"Actually, he did get the ball," said Chris. I was surprised and impressed all at the same time at my unique accomplishment. Getting the ball and the man was a rare occurrence for me during my playing days. It always seemed to end up being one or the other, but almost never both. The Kid's face turned bright red with anger and it was apparent that any buzz he had earlier had completely worn off. While we all argued on the field, I looked over towards the fence to see what was going on. It wasn't good.

Tomislav had collapsed again. Angela and the guys surrounded him. I raced over to the fence and jumped it. He was still conscious, but didn't look like he would be springing to his feet again like he had done earlier in the evening. He looked disoriented and was launching into uncontrollable coughs that sounded like he was going to pitch up one of his lungs at any moment. Angela knelt next to him and patted his face as he coughed.

She kept telling him that he was going to be okay. It wasn't something that anyone else seemed to be buying into at that point. Cowboy Chris ran up into the clubhouse and came back with a sweatshirt that Angela gently placed under her dad's head. All the color in Angela's olive-skinned face had disappeared and she looked like she was going to puke or pass out herself. I knelt down next to her and leaned in to Tomislav. Before I could say a word, Angela blurted out for somebody to call an ambulance. Suddenly, Tomislav reached up and grabbed me by the collar.

"No hospital," he demanded through a series of coughs. Angela pretended not to hear him and called out at the small group of onlookers to call an ambulance again. He reached up and tried to grab Angela's jacket sleeve with his perpetually clenched fist, but he couldn't hold onto anything with it.

"I no go anywhere," he said. Angela tried to keep her composure, but I could see her frustration and fear mounting.

"Dad, we have to get you to a hospital!"

"But the game...is not over yet," he blurted out before another brutal cough sent his head back into the folded up sweatshirt that acted as his pillow for the moment.

"The game is over dad, you're going to a hospital!"

"I will not go," he said as he reached for my jersey again and tried to pull himself up using it. I looked him in the eyes as he continued to try and pull himself up. He didn't look scared at all, he looked angry and I knew why. He didn't want his night to end like this and he wasn't about to let it. I took his hand off my jersey and gently laid it down alongside his body.

He started to reach for me again, so I stood up so he couldn't reach me anymore. He let out another succession of coughs that sounded like his whole insides might fly out of his mouth and onto the cold, hard pavement that he rested on. Then Angela stood up and looked me straight in the eye to make sure that I realized that the next thing that she said was non-negotiable.

"I'm calling an ambulance and we're getting him to the hospital," she said. I just stood there staring at her as her eyes welled up. I could tell that her mind was overrun with thoughts of her dad's life ending right before her eyes. I looked down at Tomislav who was being tended to by Goran. Tomislav continued to fight him. I would have agreed with Angela that the best thing for her dad would have been to go to the hospital if I had seen fear in his eyes, but I didn't. He would let us know what to do. And if he thought that the best thing for him would have been to get to the hospital, he would have said so.

CHAPTER 19

The ambulance idled at the entrance of the stadium as the Emergency Medical Technicians tended to Tomislav on the ground. Most of the people from the bleachers had come down and formed a tight circle around the EMTs and Tomislav despite the EMTs continued pleas to give them more room. Angela walked away from her dad while they hooked up all kinds of cords to him. I slowly and cautiously walked over to her.

"Can I talk to you?" She didn't answer, but didn't run away either. I took her by the arm and guided her away from her dad.

"But my dad."

"They've got him under control," I said in almost a whisper. She let me guide her into the locker room. Goran, Sasha, Cowboy Chris, my brother and even Mr. Nowinski followed us into the locker room as well. They came in quietly behind us and I was surprised that Angela didn't seem to mind. She started to cry a little bit, but fought feverishly to keep it together in front of all the guys in the room. She gathered herself and took a deep breath that looked like it was going to suck all the air out of the locker room. Then the silence was interrupted by her voice, which suddenly boomed.

"Don't even think of trying to convince me not to get him to the hospital!" I walked slowly around the room and then back to the door as I watched her fight with all her might to keep her composure. I knew that what I had to tell her had to happen now. She took a seat in the corner and wrapped her arms around herself.

125

"I have to help my dad! I have to go with him to the hospital!" She screamed through tears at me. Everybody else looked around the room at each other and wondered what we were doing in the locker room while Tomislav fought for his life just a few feet away.

"We should get him to hospital, no?" Goran asked.

"T-t-they could h-h-help him," pleaded Sasha. I knew that everyone thought that the logical thing to do was get him to a hospital, but they didn't realize that what was happening to Tomislav wasn't logical. It didn't make any sense at all that a cancer-riddled man who had been bedridden for weeks had just gotten up a few hours earlier and was walking around town and talking to his old friends. There was nothing logical about what was happening to Tomislav and I felt like it was the right time to tell everyone so. It was time to make it or break it.

"There's no reason to take Tomislav to the hospital, it would be a waste of time," I said. Everyone in the room stopped whatever they were doing and looked at me, drop-jawed.

"They can help him at the hospital," wailed Angela. My brother just dropped his head into his hands and started shaking it. He knew my speech wasn't going to be a big hit.

"The d-d-doctors can help," said an obviously confused Sasha through a flash-flood of tears.
Angela got up and furiously paced the room. After a few calculated steps, she charged into my face.

"Why are you doing this?" I stepped back from her, and scanned the room. Everybody besides Angela looked perplexed, she just looked angry.

"Tomislav is dying guys," I said flatly as I tried not to fall apart in front of everyone. "And the only thing the doctors can do now is help him die." Angela took a few menacing steps towards me...again.

"How do you know? Are you a doctor now?"

"No, but I've seen this before."

"Seen what?"

"What's happening to your dad right now."

"So what's happening to him now Doctor?"

"He's experiencing Stoppage Time."

"Stoppage what!? What are you talking about?" Her voice got louder and louder and her face more red with each word. I walked slowly around the cramped locker room as I weighed my words.

"It's like in soccer, you know, stoppage time. It's the time that the referee is allowed to add onto the end of the game for time wasted or injuries or long stoppages in play. Unlike all other sports, soccer counts up, not down, and the referee can add time on at his own discretion, therefore actually going past the actual time allotted." My brother shook his head in his hands as I continued. Mr. Nowinski sat motionless in his wheelchair in the corner as Cowboy Chris leaned up against the wall that led into the bathroom area. Angela charged at me again and grabbed me by the collar of my jersey. She spit all over me as she spoke, but I didn't blame her for it.

"What the hell are you talking about? Why are you making this so difficult? We need to get him to a hospital now!" She let go of me with a firm push and collapsed onto a nearby bench.

I continued on as I tried to explain what was happening to her dad.

"God tacks on more time, just like a ref does in a soccer game. He adds his own stoppage time onto the end of your life." Goran took a very long swig from the flask.

"How long does it usually last?"

"That's the thing, you never know. Only he knows," I said as I pointed up. Angela raised her reddened face out of her hands.

"How do you know any of this!?" I grabbed a small, rickety stool from the corner of the room and moved it into the middle of the room. I slowly sat on it and hoped that it wouldn't collapse under my weight. The room was completely quiet.

"My mom was bedridden for weeks and could barely talk as the cancer ravaged her body because she was so doped up on morphine to try and keep her out of pain. But one day, she suddenly started calling out for certain people and we all thought she was getting better, though there was barely anything left of her. I was so convinced that she was getting better that I went out for a while, just to try and escape the pain for a few minutes. Shortly after I left the house, she left us. But not before saying more in those few hours than she had in weeks." Angela rose from her seat and walked over to me. She laid a consoling hand on my shoulder.

"I know what happened to your mom, but that was just one time," she said. I stood up from the stool and paced the room.

"My friend's mom had been sick for months and finally went off all her medication just so she could stop being sick from it. She kept hanging on and was fine enough one night to cook dinner for her entire family after months of being extremely sick.

Everybody thought she was getting better, but later that night, she died."
Angela buried her head in her hands and cried uncontrollably. Goran went
over to her and held her tightly in his frail arms.

"You can't know that this is what's happening to my dad! Who are you
to tell us what's going on with him," she wailed at me. I knew that it was
painful for everybody to hear, but I felt that it was important that nobody get
their hopes up at a time when they were bound to be dashed sometime soon,
if not tonight. I wanted to paint a picture for everyone of how important it was
to allow Tomislav to enjoy this time he had been gifted. I continued on,
because everybody needed to hear it.

"My neighbor's dad got up in the middle of the night and went for a
walk after being bedridden for what seemed like years. She needed my help
just to get her dad back into the house, because he kept refusing to come back
inside. Later that night, he died in his sleep. Listen, I'm not trying to scare
everyone or depress everyone. I'm just trying to tell you what's going on.
Tomislav is being given this time by God to go out and enjoy life with his
friends and family and I think he should be able to take advantage of that time
to its fullest." Angela was not yet convinced.

"A few examples and now you're an expert?"

"How else do you explain it?"

"There's no way to know how much time he has left?"

"No, but it's probably not too much." Everybody dropped their heads.

"I thought it was a miracle," said Goran dejectedly as he held Angela.

"Me t-t-to," said Sasha.

"It seems like a cruel trick if you ask me, if that's even what is happening to my dad," said Angela as she politely removed Goran's arms from around her and got up again.

"I could see why you feel the way you do. It looks like it's a miracle but feels like it's a cruel trick when you realize that it's not a miracle," I said.

"So, no miracle?" Asked Goran.

"It is a miracle. But it can feel a little bit like a trick, if you don't know what's going on. That's why I'm trying to explain what is happening to Tomislav to all of you. I try to look at it more as a gift," I said. Angela's face contorted like she had just smelled some rotten food.

"A gift?"

"It's the gift of stoppage time. You aren't guaranteed to get it and it usually comes as a surprise. And I know that God would want you to enjoy it as much as you could, just like with any gift. That's why he adds that little bit of time onto the end of your life in the first place," I said. A couple heads rose slowly. Goran approached me.

"You think that is what is happening to our friend?"

"I know it is."

"So what do we do?"

"We need to help Tomislav celebrate every minute that he might have left. But we can't do that if he's in the hospital," I said.

Everybody in the room turned their attention to Angela. She then turned her attention to me and frowned through her tears. I knew that some of the anger and some of the hate that she was directing at me was her way of deflecting those same feelings from herself for bailing on her family when the going got rough.

I was willing to take it. But I wasn't willing to let it put an end to an evening I had put a lot of effort into making happen and one I know that her dad wanted to see through to completion.

"He's my dad...not yours Niko," is all she said as she stormed out of the locker room.

CHAPTER 20

I sat by myself in the corner of the locker room and listened to the sirens fade into the distance. I was pissed at myself for even trying to make the whole night happen. I was tired and angry and my whole body ached. I couldn't stomach the thought of seeing the Kid gloat over their victory and his performance, even though I did light him up good. It was over and I was on the losing end of another endeavor...again.

I didn't want to cry, I wanted to rip the locker room apart like I used to in the old days, but trying to relive the old days was what got me into my predicament in the first place. I wanted to go somewhere and hide, but I knew I couldn't do that either. When Angela left the locker room to take Tomislav to the hospital, everyone followed her out, but me. There was no way that I was going back out there to tell Tomislav that he was going to have the last night of his life cut short by an unneeded and unwanted visit to the hospital. But I knew that it was my fault that he got his hopes up in the first place.

If I would have let his family take him to the hospital earlier in the day when he first got up, he wouldn't have had to go through the whole fake night I tried to pull off on him. I couldn't stand the thought of Tomislav lying in the back of the ambulance wondering why he was going to the hospital when just minutes earlier he was enjoying a great night in a familiar place with some special people that he had known for so much of his life.

There was no way to leave the locker room without walking by everyone that was still in the stadium, so I just sat there on the bench. Suddenly, I felt nothing. I didn't feel anger or fear and happiness or sadness. I sat there, emotionless, for the first time in my life. It all turned off. I sat there staring at the small, dirty tiles until I heard the door to the locker room open. It was Cowboy Chris. He actually took his hat off as he entered the room, so I knew right then that he had some heavy stuff to lay on me. I made momentary eye contact with him and then directed my gaze back down to the small tiles on the floor.

"Waddya think we should do pardner?" I just stared at him. I felt like I didn't even have enough energy left in me to reply to his question, so I didn't.

"The Kid wants to keep playin'. He keeps sayin' that you're just scared." I shook my head a bit, shocked by the self-centeredness of the Kid. But then I thought about all the ways that I was being self-centered.

"Do ya still wanna play?" I reached down and methodically took off my left cleat. I hurled it into the shower area without looking where it landed.

Cowboy Chris looked like he was going to take a seat, but then decided otherwise. "Ya reckon we should all head to the hospital?" I took the other cleat off and threw it into the shower area as well. I peeled off my jersey, rolled it up into a ball and chucked it in his direction without ever saying a word. Cowboy Chris stood nervously in the middle of the locker room with his cowboy hat pressed against his chest. The more he spoke, the lower the tone of his voice got.

"Waddya reckon I tell everyone?"

133

I looked up at him and could tell that he had no clue what I was feeling, but I wasn't about to take it all out on him. It would have been easy to unload on the first person that walked in the door, but it wasn't his fault, it was mine. It was my fault for trying to do something special again. If I would have simply examined my own track record of significant accomplishments as an adult it would have reminded me that I had a shutout streak dating back almost a decade.

"Tell them that it's over," I said without looking him in the eye.

"Ya serious?" I never answered him. After standing in front of me for what must have been five minutes, Cowboy Chris walked out of the locker room. He optimistically left the door propped open. Maybe he thought that it would get me up off my butt just to see how many people were still waiting on me in the stadium. I just sat there and stared at the fog rolling onto the field. A light rain was falling and I wished for a moment that the end of my life would come before the end of Tomislav's. I let out a little laugh as I watched the rain start to fall harder and harder. It was one of those laughs that you let out when there's nothing left to do; when all the crying and screaming and yelling just won't do the moment justice. The kind of laugh that says, 'you got me, I give up.' I decided to take a shower and was pleasantly surprised when the water actually came out hot.

After a long shower, I slowly dried off. Instead of sitting back down I went over and stood in the open doorway. The rain was coming down pretty heavily and the fog was coming in thick. The cold didn't bother me at all, I just stood there in the doorway, in nothing but a towel, wondering what was going to happen next.

The Gift of Stoppage Time

Nobody could see me because I was behind the propped open door in the doorway, but I could still hear plenty of people milling around. It sounded like both teams were still on the field knocking the ball around, but not actually playing a game.

I stared blankly out into the small warm-up area behind the goal and the old, beat up snack bar. Good memories buzzed through my head, but were quickly flooded out of my mind by the painful memories from a night that looked to be all but over with. I looked through the twenty-foot-tall chain link fence over at the Rec Center that sat just across a narrow street from the open end of the stadium as an ambulance slowly rolled by with its sirens off. I refused to get my hopes up and instead figured that its services were needed by some other poor soul in town. I went back inside the locker room and took a seat on the bench. I sat there staring out at the rain for minutes. My eyelids felt heavy and I decided to let myself doze off. I closed my eyes. I wanted to get lost in my dreams for just a few minutes. I was so tired. I wanted my mind to take me to happier times, so I let myself go.

Time was not of the essence anymore and I felt like I could finally relax without losing out on something. I could hear myself snoring lightly as I dreamt about playing in a packed stadium in Europe with thousands of people watching my every move. My model girlfriend was sitting in my personal luxury box with a handful of my friends from the States. Just as I was about to score the game-winning goal, my dream was interrupted by an all-too-familiar voice.

"Niko...Niko!" I opened my eyes to see Angela. I blinked extremely hard a few times to make sure that what I saw was real and not just some figment of my imagination.

135

She was standing in the doorway with her hair wetand her eye makeup smeared from not only the rain, but obviously a steady stream of tears.

"Can I come in?" I nodded her in while I tried to get myself completely out of my dream. She came in and closed the door behind her. Then she walked right towards me. She stopped a few feet shy of me and pointed to my gut, which was protruding like I had stuffed a bowling ball under the skin of my belly.

"Twins?"

"No, just old age."

"You're not that old."

"I'm an old soul."

"No you're not!"

"Then I'm simply a loser," I said dejectedly.

"You're not that either. You're the farthest thing from a loser that I know." I wondered what had triggered her sudden change of emotions, but I also didn't care too much. I was just enjoying her being civil to me again.

"Can I sit with you?"

"Sure," I said without hesitation. I didn't know how to even start, so I waited to see if she would, which she did. She sat down and turned her gaze in my direction. Her eyes were looking right into me, not through me. It felt weird. It felt way too intimate considering the fact that I hadn't seen her in years and was now having heart to heart conversations with her on an almost hourly basis. I remembered her looks from so many years ago. Her slightly crooked dark eyes used to be able to shoot holes in any of my little white lies with a single glance.

I stopped slouching and pulled myself up so that I leaned straight up against the tile wall. She tilted her head as she spoke and lowered her tone so much that her words were barely audible.

"Can I ask you something?" I nodded, already seemingly at a loss for words, which wasn't a good thing.

"Why is this so important to you?"

"Why's what?"

"This whole thing with my dad...this game...this night," she said. I scooted away from her a little bit so that I could gauge her body's reaction to my answer.

"It's not just about me Angela. In this life, I believe that you only get one chance to do things right the first time. When my mom struggled for her life, I know that I didn't do things right. But I just didn't know what was going on back then. The night she died, I left the house to go to the movies with my friends because I thought she was getting better and I felt like I needed a break from all the pain. In reality, she was enjoying the last few minutes of her life and I wasn't there for that. I would have had a break from the pain just a few hours later if I just hadn't been so selfish. I should have been thinking about her pain the whole time, not mine. It's tough, because when we are forced to sit there and watch a loved one struggle for their lives, we get all caught up in our pain and our feelings. But sometimes we lose sight of their feelings, their pain, what they might want." Angela laid a hand on my shoulder and her eyes welled up.

"You did what you could," she said. I didn't want to get mad at her or disagree with her, but I knew that it was critical that she understood where I was coming from to understand why the night was so important to me.

137

"No I didn't. I could have done more. You can always do more. With your dad, I'm just trying to help. But this night isn't about me trying to absolve myself of any regret I have over how I handled my mom's situation. I know that my mom has forgiven me for what I didn't do to help her, and I'm sure that she knows I enjoyed all the time I had with her. But it still hurts. Your dad is a very good man and has helped me through many times in my life when I needed it. Now, I just want to help him the same way he used to help me, even if it's just for one last night."

"So this has nothing to do with you? It's all about him?" It felt like a trick question, even though I knew she didn't mean it like that. Because no matter what we all say, when we help other people, we're always helping ourselves too. But there's nothing wrong with that. In fact, that's the way it is supposed to be.

"It's doesn't have anything to do with me," I said. She took my hand with her hand and squeezed it tightly.

"Okay, I believe you."

"Thanks."

"How badly do you want to kick that punk's butt?"

"What?"

"I brought my dad back...he insisted that we come back. He said that you never leave a game early unless it's for something very, very serious."

"So how's he feeling?"

"The same. The EMTs wanted to take him to the hospital, but he insisted and got pretty upset in the back of the ambulance. They finally relented and turned the ambulance around."

138

"But I thought you wanted him to go to the hospital?"

"Yeah I did Niko. But it's like you just said, it's not about what I want. It's what my dad wants and what he wants tonight is to watch the end of this game with his friends."

"And family," I added. She smiled and then started to cry. She leaned in to me and grabbed me tightly around the shoulders. I extended my arms around her slight frame and then engulfed her in the same kind of intestine-jarring hug that she had me in. Her body started to jerk and shudder because she was crying so hard. I held her tightly, but didn't cry. It was her time to let it all out and I wanted to be there for her. She buried her face in my neck and I wanted so much to tell her that it would be okay, but that would have been a lie. She knew what the end result of the whole evening was going to be, it was just a matter of accepting it and moving forward.

"He told me how much he loved me," she said through a barrage of tears.

"Of course he loves you."

"He told me how when I was born one of the guys ragged on him for not having a boy and he knocked the guy off the side of the boat and into the ocean with one punch."

"That sounds just like your dad."

"He said that all he ever wanted in his life was for me to be happy."

"I'm sure that's all he wants...and to watch a good game of soccer from time to time," I said. She pulled away from me and mixed in a laugh in with all her tears.

"I don't remember the last time he told me he loved me," she said. I quickly wiped a tear that welled in the corner of my eye. I gently approached her face with my hand and wiped some tears from her face.

"He's just an old-school guy. That's how they are."

"How's that?"

"They're just hard, you know? Everything he did in his life was for you and your mom. He used to always rave about how beautiful you were and how good you were doing in school and how he would crush anyone who treated you wrongly."

"Really?"

"Absolutely. But when you left, he had no choice but to try and turn some of his feelings for you off, because it hurt him so badly that you were gone."

"He never even called."

"He just wanted to see you Angela."

She placed both of her hands on my cheeks and I was suddenly reminded of when I tried to kiss her after my mom died and she pulled away and asked me what the heck I was doing. I smiled at her and she smiled back.

"Will you still play?"

"Sure, but can I ask you something?" She frantically wiped tears from her eyes with the back of her hand. I stood up in front of her and pretended to be ready to whip off my towel to help her with it.

"Here, use this to wipe your eyes," I said.

"Don't even think about it," she said through more laughter and tears.

"Whatever happened with that guy?" The guy I was referring to was a trust fund jerk she met in college that pretended to be an artist and made her stay on the East Coast to be around his friends and family and to isolate her away from hers.

"I don't know how he's doing."

"Weren't you married to him?"

"We were engaged for a while, but when my dad got sick he started freaking out when I mentioned that I might move home to be with him."

"So you broke up?"

"Well, sort of. I moved out of his place and got my own place and I just started thinking about how I was giving up everything out here to help him live his dream out there, but I wasn't living any of mine."

"That sounds familiar," I said.

"So that's how you ended up back here too?"

"In a roundabout way...yeah. There's something that I realized after all these years Angela. When you're in a relationship, it's important to give of yourself...but not up yourself." She sat there mesmerized for a moment, as she pondered the thought.

"I definitely gave up myself for him."

"And that's wrong, but it's never too late to get yourself back." I think that she was taken aback by all my new philosophies. Back when we dated or whatever we called it in high school, my life was soccer, soccer and more soccer.

"I want myself back Niko. Will you help me do that?"

"You know I will."

She squeezed my face and pulled it into hers. I knew that if I kissed her there would be no way that I could go back on the field and play an effective game of soccer, so I leaned away from her. She opened her eyes. They were filled with more surprise than disappointment.

"You're kidding, right?"

"No...you remember...soccer first. It's always soccer first," She patted my cheek more firmly than a love tap and gritted her teeth momentarily.

"You better win this game or my dad will be pissed," she said as she snuck a quick peck on my cheek. Her lips felt as soft as ever. Energy shot through my body from head to toe.

CHAPTER 21

Tomislav was leaning against the fence when I came out of the locker room, which I didn't think was a very good idea. But when I brought up the option of sitting in the bleachers, he brushed me off with a wave of his hand and a brief lecture.

"In forty years of coming to this field, I never sit in those bleachers," he said as he vigorously wagged a finger at the bleachers like they were some kind of evil. I didn't know exactly what happened in that ambulance, but something did, because Tomislav suddenly appeared to be very full of life. I scanned the bleachers quickly and noticed that many people had left. The guys from the docks had bailed, probably to meet up with us later. An old man and woman still remained, but were playing cards with each other, straddling the benches, using the cold metal between them as a table. My eyes continued to roam the sparse crowd when they came upon a familiar figure.

He was wearing a raincoat and had an umbrella opened above him to protect his full head of transplanted hair from what was now just a very light rain.

We made eye contact, but he didn't react.. I turned to the field and sought out my brother who was standing in goal doing jumping jacks to try and stay warm. My brother caught my glare and shrugged his shoulders semi-apologetically. My brother was probably more excited to have our dad come see him play under the lights than he was interested in helping mend a relationship that had faded many years ago.

Angela stood along the fence between her dad and uncle with her arms draped around both of them. She looked happy and that made me happy, though I was a little worried that I had enough energy to make a difference in the last twenty minutes that were left to play after sitting dormant in the locker room for close to an hour. It was basically like starting a whole new game again, but with only twenty-minutes left and down by a goal. Everyone seemed to be more relieved than excited to see me, but that was fine too, because I was feeling pretty good. Cowboy Chris looked the most relieved when he came up to me and grabbed me in a big bear hug at midfield in front of everyone.

"I knew you'd come back," he said through wet eyes.

"Just make sure the breaks go my way," I said loud enough so the Kid could hear.

I knew the comment would wind him up, but that's exactly what I wanted. Win, lose or draw, I wanted the last few minutes of the game to be memorable for everyone involved. The rain had subsided, but a cold wind had picked up and was whipping up from the harbor through the field. The fog kept rolling in and out of the field, hiding the houses in the surrounding neighborhoods from us and making it seem like we were all alone.

The Kid must have been going nuts trying to keep all the trash he wanted to talk bottled up inside his skinny frame while the game was put on hold. He crossed over from his half of the field and placed a hard hand on my shoulder, turning me away from Cowboy Chris.

"Yo...you got any legs left, old man?" I took his hand off my shoulder and delivered a playful, back-handed slap across his chest.

The Gift of Stoppage Time

"I got new ones. So watch out." I knew I was running out of time, but it didn't worry me. I knew that a lot could happen in way less than a half an hour in soccer and so did everybody else that was standing over at the fence. Their encouragement grew louder and louder as Cowboy Chris raised the whistle to start the game...again.

My first touch was a nice, solid one that kept the ball close enough to my feet that I could do anything that I wanted with it. I whipped a perfectly bent ball with the outside of my left foot to the feet of my winger without making him move an inch. Instead of letting him take the ball up field, I checked in to him and demanded the ball back. He played me a lazy, bouncy pass that wasn't even coming close to my feet. I was forced to lunge for it with my right leg and was unceremoniously hacked across the shin by the Kid as I finally made contact with the ball. I rolled over in pain and clutched my shin. I knew that he got me good, but I didn't want to go after him. I just wanted a second to collect my thoughts before I got up.

"Stay down old man," he said as he stood over me.

"That was a love tap on this field Kid, you'll have to do better than that." I got up and took a look at my shin. The hit had raised a golf-ball sized lump in the middle of my shin. It hurt, but it made me feel more awake.

I always used to feel more in the game after a couple of good hits, although this time was different because I was on the receiving end. But that was okay, because not only did it get me back into the game within seconds, it got my mean streak back in tact; and that was a part of my game I could never do without.

I took the ball and set it down for the free kick that I was awarded by Cowboy Chris for the reckless, stupid and ultimately relatively harmless foul committed by the Kid.

I pumped the ball deep down into their penalty box. I hit it too deep and with hardly any pace. Their goalkeeper gobbled it up easily before anyone on my team could get a head to it. Instead of punting the ball away though, their keeper rolled the ball out to the Kid who was demanding it at the edge of the penalty area, which was a dangerous place to get the ball from the keeper at any time during the game, let alone with only minutes remaining and a slim one-goal advantage. I figured I might as well make a run at him and force him to do something stupid with the ball, which he did.

Instead of turning the ball out or clearing it off to the side as I approached, the Kid decided to put his goalkeeper in a precarious position by playing him a way-too-slow back pass. I chugged past the Kid at less than the speed of sound and continued on, hoping to poke the ball past the keeper who was having a hard time controlling the ball at his feet. He fumbled with the ball so much that he finally just swung his leg wildly at it and launched the ball out of bounds over the byline. I had earned a corner kick for our team and I was proud of it. The Kid dropped into the box to mark me after giving his keeper an earful about his inability to control what should have never been a back pass in the first place.

I lined up at the top of the penalty box like I always used to in anticipation of the corner kick. I liked to start my runs way up high on the top of the box because it made it harder for guys to knock you off your run and it made it easier for me to follow the flight of the ball and to time my one-footed take off.

The Gift of Stoppage Time

Years of having guys grab my jersey and step on my feet so that I couldn't jump taught me to never stand flat-footed before I made my run. The Kid walked up next to me and took a finger-full of my jersey. Then he stood flat-footed as he waited for the next bit of action to take place. Even though he was doing everything wrong to prepare for the ensuing corner kick, he still had the guts to talk trash.

"Where you think you're going?"

"Better have more than that to try and stop me," I said as I inspected his scrawny hand as it clutched the sleeve of my jersey.

There was no chance he was going to be able to hold me or bump me with the positioning he had taken up. His body faced the ball, not me and his hand barely had any grasp of my jersey at all. The point of grabbing players wasn't to figure out what type of fabric the jersey was made of, it was to keep the player from going where they wanted to in the proper amount of time. It was one of those small details of the game that the Kid never learned on the club soccer fields in the suburbs where looking good was valued much more than actually playing well. It was typical defending from a guy who thought that the defending part of the game was a total waste of time. That's why he was always a forward and why guys who thought that way always tended to be forwards. Xavier waltzed over to the Kid and tried to switch men with him.

The Kid wouldn't have any of it as he was bent on denying me the game-tying goal. I knew that if my teammate could flight it into the right spot, I could get to it. I placed my hand on the hand of the Kid just as my teammate sent the ball flying in our direction. I threw the Kid's hand off my jersey and then threw him out of the way and onto the ground.

147

He screamed for a call, but there was no way Cowboy Chris was going to whistle something so innocent at this stage of the game. The ball had a decent bend to it and was out-swinging away from the keeper and into my path. I got to right about the penalty spot and took off of my left foot. Their goalkeeper scrambled at the last minute to get off of his line and into the path of the ball. It was too late. I met the ball with the bridge of my nose.

It rocketed towards the empty goal but rose just enough at the last second to hit the crossbar and come back into play. Dave the nerd was credited with the game-tying goal for simply standing close enough to the goal that the ball came off the post, hit him in the face and rolled into an empty net. My nose throbbed mightily, but I didn't care. I was happy for Dave and my team. I wanted to take off towards the crowd, but didn't have the chance to get there. My teammates mobbed me and Dave right there in front of the goal. The assist felt great, my nose did not. Blood trickled out of it and I wiped it clean with sleeve of my jersey. Then I continued on celebrating with my teammates. I could hear Angela, Tomislav and the guys cheering for us over at the fence, but my teammates wouldn't let me out of their grasp. They patted my head, hugged me and slapped my back. It felt more like I was getting jumped into a gang for the first time than being congratulated for helping create a pretty sweet game-tying goal.

As we worked our way out of their penalty box, the Kid stormed past me towards their goalkeeper who was still lying on the ground after colliding with some players. He berated his own goalkeeper for giving up the goal even though it was he who lost his track of the man he was supposed to mark. I couldn't resist another opportunity to teach the Kid another lesson in soccer life.

I eluded some overly-affectionate teammates for the moment and called out to him as he rained down insults on his keeper who was still writhing around on the ground in pain.

"I was your man...not his," I said.

"Mind your own business," he shot back at me. I stormed over at him, despite my teammates' attempts to simply get me back to midfield for the kickoff.

"This is my business! I got away from you, not him!" I shouted in his face. "They should all be yelling at you, because you're the culprit, not him!" Some of his teammates nodded in agreement at my rationale and told the Kid to back off. The Kid was pissed at his goalkeeper, but he hadn't even scored a goal yet and I had a couple of assists and my team back in the game. The Kid looked like he was going to say something back to me, but then he relented and instead got the ball out of the back of the net and started to run it back out to midfield.

"That's right, pick it out," I said arrogantly.

"Don't worry...I will...because it's on!" I tried to knock the ball out of his hands, but was unsuccessful. Cowboy Chris didn't know whether to blow the whistle or just let us keep having a go at each other, so he just stood there.

I was in no hurry to get back to my side of the field; they couldn't kick off until we were all over on our own side anyway. I shook a triumphant fist towards my fans as I strolled back onto my side of the field.

"Looks like we have a game on our hands," I said to the Kid as I defiantly stepped in between him and his teammate who were all lined up for the kickoff. The score was all knotted up at 3-3 and time was running out quickly.

Dave's goal and the ensuing celebration had sapped some energy that would have been better used at something more effective, like defending the last few minutes of the game, but it was all well worth it. I glanced over at the fence to see Tomislav still standing. He looked at me and nodded ever-so-slightly. He was never one to get outwardly emotional when he was watching games because he had been in so many as a player himself. Angela either had too much to drink or was falling for me again, because she even blew me a kiss when I looked over. Tomislav gave me a disheartened look when he realized that I took my gaze off of him and onto his beautiful daughter. It wasn't because Angela was his daughter and he didn't want me to be with her, nothing could be further from the truth, he had always hoped we would end up together.

His look of disappointment was due to the fact that my affection for him being side-tracked by his one and only child. Getting side-tracked by women was something that not only was forbidden at Daniel's Field, it actually got guys cut from their teams. Team owners would cast off players guilty of casting an affectionate wave or wink towards their significant other instead of fulfilling their roles on the field.

Softies were never welcome at Daniel's Field and were always given their little pillow and told to take their services elsewhere once their dedication to the game was shown to be less than one-hundred percent of what they had in their body. I knew that the Kid was looking to get back at me quickly, so right off the kickoff I stormed up into him before he even had time to get his head up and delivered a heavy forearm just under his chin. He crumpled to the ground in a heap and stayed down, holding his throat.

"It's starting to feel like the good old days again," I said as he tried to capture his breath. I extended my hand down to help him up, but he smacked it away. I laughed and ran back on defense. I had caught my second wind and was running without too much labor. After a few runs up and down the field for both teams, I asked Cowboy Chris how much time was left.

"Not much," is all he told me as he struggled to keep up with the play.

The Kid picked up a ball at midfield and worked his way through our porous defense. I had a shot at him, but it was just inside the penalty box and I didn't want to commit a foul, so I let him get by. He ran in on my brother who charged off of his line at the Kid as best he could. The Kid smartly wound up to shoot, but then tapped the ball by my brother once my brother took flight at him. The Kid did another smart thing and dragged his feet. My brother couldn't help but hit the Kid's feet. The Kid went sprawling to the cold, wet grass on contact and Cowboy Chris was left with no option but to call a penalty kick with only minutes left on the clock. The Kid jumped to his feet and got the ball from out of bounds. He hustled over to the penalty spot and placed it on the ground. Xavier went over to him and urged him not to take it.

"The guy who got fouled should never take the kick," is all he said and he was right. It was widely believed that the guy who got fouled was always too emotional to take it and it was good old soccer lore that stated the fouled guy who insisted on taking the penalty kick always seemed to miss. The Kid blew him off and vehemently brushed him aside. I stood on top of the box and wondered which way he would go.

Then it struck me that since the Kid hadn't played in so long he'd probably just try to bang it right up the middle in the hopes that my brother would guess first and launch his body for one of the corners. The Kid took a lot of steps back from the ball and I knew then that he was planning on banging it home, or at least trying to. My brother stood in goal, adjusting his goggles, headband and kneepads as Cowboy Chris waited for him to be ready. I whistled out to my brother and when we made eye contact I motioned with both hands for him to stay put.

I don't know if he understood what I meant by my signal, but he stayed in the middle of the goal and did not move to either side when the Kid unleashed a bomb of a knuckleball shot at him. The ball rose towards my brother's face and he was lucky enough to get his hands up in front of his face at the last possible second to keep the ball from blasting his goggles into the back of his eye sockets and to send the ball up into the crossbar and back into play. I reacted a little late, but it was still enough time to get into the box and into the Kid. As the ball dropped out of the sky, the Kid tried to volley it, but

I slid into him at the last second and poked the ball away as he swung wildly at nothing but air. He cussed loudly as his leg followed through so hard that it sent him airborne. He landed awkwardly on his back and let out a terrible scream. Everyone stopped because of the scream, not the fact that he might have been hurt. Screams were never heard at Daniel's Field. Maybe yells, but not screams...ever! Tomislav and the guys at the fence had a good laugh at the Kid's expense.

The Kid pretended not to hear all of the people who were clowning on him. Instead, he shot to his feet and ran to get the ball to take the corner kick after appealing for another penalty kick.

Cowboy Chris ignored his pleas and pointed to his watch. The score was tied 3-3 and I wasn't about to let my team lose in the waning seconds.

"How much time we got?"

"Not much," Cowboy Chris told me.

"Minutes?"

"Seconds actually."

"Keep it going, you're the ref, the amount of stoppage time is totally up to you," I said.

"You can't get to the other end of the field in seconds?"

"Not anymore," I said with a laugh. Cowboy Chris slapped my back as I made a run for the near post to cut the ball off. The Kid placed the ball for the corner kick. There was barely any room for a player to back up from the ball, so all the Kid had was a one-step approach. He tried to hammer the ball near-post like a typical ball-hog. I cleared his weak cross up the field and took off on a sprint towards the ball. There were only a few more minutes, at best, to break the tie.

I knew that nobody would go home happy with a tie, so it was all or none. I was more willing to go for the win and leave ourselves exposed to a last-minute counter-attack than to sit back and grind out the time for a tie. My logic defied conventional soccer wisdom, but I knew that nothing about the game and the whole night was conventional or followed any type of logic anyway, so I figured what the heck. Xavier collected the ball and tried to hammer it back into our end, but Dave jumped and blocked his attempted clearance.

The ball squirted behind their defense and way back into their end of the field. Even though I was getting closer to their half, I was getting farther away from the ball. Chills went up my spine with every step as my body fought cramps and overall extreme fatigue, but it felt good to let the adrenaline take my body over as I sprinted as fast as I could up field and into the howling wind.

Another one of their defenders tried to clear the ball and again the ball deflected off of one of my out-of-control forwards. The ball flew way up in the air and started to get blown out of their end by the wind. Instead of going up for the loose-ball header, I let two other players battle it out and waited patiently for the ball to drop into my path. It did and I settled it quickly and took off at their defense that was spaced out just enough so I could weave in between a few of them without too much fuss. I reached the top of the penalty box and saw that another defender was recovering from the outside and was more than likely going to be able to cut me off before I got one-on-one with the goalkeeper. I put the ball on my left foot because I had always been able to put a good amount of power and also some movement on the ball with that foot as opposed to my right foot.

I took a quick glance at where the goalkeeper was and then put my head down. For a moment I thought about faking the shot and letting the defender fly right by me, but I knew the chances of me finishing my run with a nice soft touch around the goalkeeper at the end of it was highly unlikely. I put my head down, locked my ankle and curled my toes, then hit through the ball as hard as I could.

The Gift of Stoppage Time

The second I made contact with the ball I knew that something special was going to happen to it. The ball exploded off my foot and started off going right at the goalkeeper. But then it started to tail away from him and I could see from the look in his eyes that he was going to have a hard time getting to it. The ball continued to tail away from him towards the far corner of the goal. I slowed down as everything slowed down around me and went totally quiet. The ball kept tailing away from the keeper and his outstretched arms and then continued on until it hit the upper corner of the post and ricocheted into the goal. It finally came to rest beautifully in the back corner of the net, much to the goalkeeper's dismay.

The quiet was interrupted by the raucous cheers of my teammates and the crowd. A chill rocked my body from head to toe. I looped my run past the keeper and back towards my people who were standing over at the fence. I pumped both my fists out in front of me as I charged towards them at a speed I didn't know that I had in me yelling something at the top of my lungs to nobody in particular. It was my moment and I wanted to share it with everyone. I reached the fence and heard Cowboy Chris whistle three times to signal the end of the match. Angela was jumping up and down with her arms raised triumphantly over her head, screaming for joy, totally lost in the moment.

Tomislav stood there, holding onto the fence with both hands, shaking his head. As I got closer to him I could see that he was smiling, obviously blown away by the pure audacity of my game-winning goal. Goals like the one I had just scored were indescribable simply with words. They demanded more than that and raw emotions were the only thing that could do my game-winning stroke of soccer brilliance justice.

155

The Gift of Stoppage Time

Just before I reached Angela and the guys at the fence, I was unceremoniously blind-sided by my brother and half-a-dozen of my new teammates. The first hit from my brother planted me face up on the ground with him squarely on top of me. He yelled and screamed incomprehensible rumblings of our triumph while unintentionally spitting all over me as the rest of the guys piled on. It didn't feel good, but I was forced to forgive them for their unbridled affection towards me, since it was undoubtedly the biggest win the guys had ever been a part of. As everyone piled on me, I could see out of the corner of my eye a body doubled over in agony on the field. It was the Kid and he was taking the loss harder than any one of his teammates. I tried to make eye contact with him, but he wouldn't allow it. He laid there face down and with his head in his hands, apparently crying. I didn't believe it at first, but as he rose to his feet I saw that his face was contorted in anguish that couldn't be feigned. I felt bad for a moment, but then went back to trying to figure out how to get a dozen, overweight and sweaty grown men off of me.

My teammates slowly piled off of me and were frantically embracing each other all around me. I was left all alone for a brief moment on the wet field to catch my breath. I propped myself up and was sitting there motionless with my arms wrapped around my knees.

I watched the Kid slowly trudge off the field, his body jerking as he cried out loud to nobody in particular. I looked over at the fence and saw Cowboy Chris in a full embrace with Angela as she seemed to be trying to peel him off of her. I noticed that most of the couple dozen people in the crowd were on their feet, observing the celebrations on the field.

The Gift of Stoppage Time

The dark figure with the umbrella wasn't there anymore and it didn't bother me a bit. I could see that Tomislav and the guys were impatiently waiting for me over at the fence. I wish they would have come onto the field to celebrate with me, but I knew they wouldn't. That was part of one of their old-school traditions as well. They believed that only the players and managers celebrated on the field, because it was their time and place to be together, while everyone else waited for them to leave that sacred, beat-up patch of bermuda grass that we all used to call home every Sunday.

I looked back over my shoulder at the goal I just scored on. The ball still sat there in the back corner of the net, all by itself. I wanted to go over and pick it up. But I didn't want to grab it and go home. I wanted to play more soccer. As tired and beat up and exhausted and burned-out as I felt, I realized that the last thing I wanted was for the game to be over with. The fog was rolling in so thick that it was hard to even see the lights that hovered above me. The wind was whipping up off the harbor so hard that it had the light posts were swaying slightly to an unheard beat. It was cold and damp and getting late, but I felt like I had another half left in me. I might have, because I only played a half and that was something I definitely wasn't used to. Back in the day, I started every game on the field and finished the same way. I was a full-time grinder and proud of it.

I thought I did well in the role I was forced to play, but could feel my body yearning for more of the old days...the good old days. The pain I was feeling was the good kind of pain where your body knew just how hard it was pushed and got sore on purpose so that you knew just how hard you played it.

157

My Achilles throbbed, my neck was getting stiff, my hamstrings and calves teased me with spasms and the small of my back burned like somebody was prodding it with a hot iron. I hurt physically, but felt great emotionally. My body was letting out all of those chemicals that it's supposed to when you treat it right. And for the first time in many years, I gave it what it had been yearning for. But most of all, it was over. I had set out to do it and somehow, someway, got the game done. Playing a big part of it was the icing on the cake, but I was mostly glad that I pulled it off and didn't disappoint Tomislav. That would have been a disaster. It was funny to think back to how it even all came together, which was only a few hours earlier, but seemed like ages ago. The relief of having pulled it off would have been more overwhelming if it weren't for all the adrenaline that pumped through my veins after scoring one of the best goals of my life.

Before I was able to get too nostalgic, I noticed that the guys from the other team were slowly making their way through my team and shaking their hands. I gathered myself and slowly started trying to get myself to my feet. Xavier walked over to me and extended me his hand. I grabbed it tightly and he helped me to my feet. "That goal was sick," he said.

"Thanks."

"You ever play anywhere?" He asked. I knew he wanted to hear that I played somewhere big-time, so I didn't even bother.

"I used to kick it around from time to time," I said humbly.

"I thought we had you guys."

"You guys played well, it was a tough one out there," I said. He extended his hand to me again and we shook. He pulled me in for one of those man-buddy hugs.

"Thanks for having us out here."

"No problem. Thank you guys for coming out."

"You gonna set up another game soon?" I looked at the two teams that were shaking hands and even sharing a few hugs. I looked up again to see all the different people who somehow turned out for the game still standing in the bleachers. I saw Angela and the guys replaying parts of the game to each other as they waited on all of us. I wanted to tell him that I was going to set up another game very soon, but I couldn't. I really didn't know if a night like the night we were having would ever come around again. But that would be okay too, because I didn't know if I could ever put myself through what I was going through tonight.

"Maybe, we'll have to see," I said.

"About what?"

"Lots of things." He must have been able to tell that he was ruining my natural buzz because he backed off. He slapped my shoulder and made his way through the rest of what were now officially my teammates.

I gingerly worked my way past my still-celebrating teammates and over to the fence. I noticed that Tomislav and the guys weren't there anymore. Only Angela and Chris were left.

"Everything okay?"

"Yeah, they're all waiting in the locker room," said Angela with a big smile. I started towards the locker room, when I was interrupted by a smack to the back of the head. Cowboy Chris stood there with his arms extended wide.

"I told ya that ya were gonna play pardner!"

"Unfortunately, you were right."

"Unfortunately my butt pardner! Ya tore it up out there tonight!"

"I guess I did...didn't I?"

"Yeah ya did pardner, that was old school you."

"I like that me."

 "Ya lit that kid up like a Christmas tree."

"I did get him pretty good, huh?"

"I reckon that his New Year's resolution is going to be to try and get rid of all the pain ya inflicted on him with that tackle by next year." I felt a little bit badly about the whole episode after knowing how low the Kid's life was before I brought him into the game. Unfortunately, he was leaving the game in an even lower state than when he arrived at it. I felt bad for a split second, but also realized it would have been easy for him to not talk so much trash too. I scanned the field and bleachers for him to no avail. I wondered if he was even in the locker room. But I wasn't about to go into the losing team's locker room, at least not before I went into mine. Then I heard Angela's voice.

"Hey, old man!" I turned around to look and make sure she was talking to me, because there were a lot of old men around.

"I know you're not calling me old."

"Sure I am. Nice game tough guy." Her smile was as wide as I had seen it all night and it made me feel good at first, but then scared that the whole night was going to hit her even harder now that there was some hope sprinkled into it.

CHAPTER 22

The last time I chugged a beer right after a game, it felt like everything in my body, from my kidneys to my eyelids, were cramping up on me. So when I walked into what was a very celebratory locker room, I was less than amused when Goran rushed up to me with an ice-cold can of beer clasped tightly in his skinny, shivering fingers and adamantly thrust it into my stomach.

"The MVP, the MVP," he chanted with as much energy as his little body would allow itself to expend. The rest of my teammates as well as Tomislav and Sasha joined in the chorus. I clasped the beer tightly in my hands, which were shaking just a little bit, and popped it open. The old, stuffy, locker room erupted in another chorus of cheers. I stared at the opening of the can dead on for a moment, and then, with total disregard for what I knew it was going to do to me, slammed the entire thing without even as much as taking a breath. I crumpled up the can and threw it triumphantly into the shower area. My new teammates rushed me and surrounded me with their beers as we all joined in a synchronized jump while we chanted the only chorus we all knew together and could recite to perfection and without much effort.

"Ole...ole, ole, ole...ole, ole."

"Ole...ole, ole, ole...ole, ole."

"Ole...ole, ole, ole...ole, ole."

It went on for minutes, or at least a minute, until that all too familiar feeling invaded my insides again. I tried to fight it as I jumped as high as I could with my arms draped firmly around my brother's and Sasha's shoulders, but it didn't work. I let go of both of them and darted to the bathroom to toss up what was just seconds ago, a perfectly cold brew. When I returned to the changing area from the bathroom stalls, I was met with some concerned looks from my teammates. Tomislav, Goran and Sasha let out raucous laughs as they inspected my greenish exterior. The old-school guys always loved it when the younger guys did something stupid and I had done something extraordinarily stupid again. And throwing up a celebratory beer in the locker room definitely fit the bill.

I let out a little barf-laced laugh and was once again met by Goran who knifed his way through my teammates and presented me with yet another cold brew. There was no way I intended to drink another one until I looked over at Tomislav, who was leaning on the trainer's table, and not looking half bad. He smiled and nodded for me to drink it while he held his own brew, and I knew that at that point, the choice not to try it again had just been taken away from me.

"No jumping afterwards this time," I said. Then I popped it open and guzzled it again. This time it hit my stomach and decided to stay put for a while. My teammates, led by my brother, rushed me again with their beers in hand and showered me with ice cold beer. They rubbed it into my hair and clipped me a few times around the head with their cans, but I didn't care.

Everyone launched their empty, crumpled up cans into the shower area like I did and went back to the cooler that had somehow found its way into the locker room since the game had ended.

The Gift of Stoppage Time

I sat on the training table next to where Tomislav and the guys stood. They all patted me on the back as we all sipped our beers. Tomislav raised his beer to mine and we silently toasted each other. My silent toast was to Tomislav for still being there despite his failing health, while I guessed Tomislav was toasting something more along the lines of how hard I smacked that Kid with my slide tackle. Our special moment was unceremoniously interrupted when I heard my brother's booming voice over everyone else's.

"You lost?"

I looked at where my brother was directing his question. It was to the half-open locker room door. From my angle, I couldn't see who it was, but I could tell that my brother could.

"Is Niko around?" The voice was all too familiar to me and my brother. It was a pleasant surprise to see my brother play bodyguard for me. He continued his interrogation of the Kid as the locker room became eerily quiet.

"Maybe...why?"

The Kid poked his head into the most celebratory locker room in town and frantically tried to find me. He spotted me quickly enough, but all I did was shrug my shoulders. I wasn't about to let him off the hook that easy.

"What do you need Kid?" My brother asked him. The Kid turned his eyes back to my brother who approached him at the door before he could even think of completely entering our locker room. My brother flung the door open. It left the Kid standing there, red eyes and all...in front of my whole team and a few extremely loyal fans.

The Gift of Stoppage Time

"Hey man, it's cool. I just wanted to tell him that he had a good game," he said meekly. My brother blocked his path into our locker room and eye-balled him from head to toe, looking for some sincerity in his voice or demeanor. Gone was the punk kid who had gone into the game thinking he was a world-beater. The puffed-out chest was replaced by a slouched and slightly crooked stance. He bowed his head in deference to his victors and fumbled his fingers in front of himself as he waited for my gatekeeper's verdict. All that was left of him was a dinged-up young man who learned the hard way that respect was earned and simply not demanded.

Nobody quite knew what to do. It was hardly the Kid we had been subjected to for the last few hours of our lives. Everyone looked over at me for a decision, but I wasn't sure which was going to be the right one. I felt that if I let him in my teammates would admonish me for being soft. But if I turned him away they would forever remember what an unforgiving hard-ass I was. And I knew that wasn't me either. I competed harder than most, but when it was over, it was over, sans maybe a brief skirmish on the way to the locker rooms after the game. But I knew that what we all wanted and what we all loved was the competition that the game rewarded us with and when it was over, it was a time to either celebrate or wallow. The Kid was being forced to wallow, but it wasn't entirely his fault, it was mine. I'm the one who buried the world-class goal that put them under and sent us off that field victorious. So why should I have been bitter towards him at all?

I nodded for my brother to let him in. He slowly walked in as he cautiously inspected the room, wondering if we were all suddenly going to pounce on him and rough him up for being such a trash-talker out on the field.

164

The Gift of Stoppage Time

In all my years of playing at Daniel's Field, I never walked into an opposing locker room. In fact, the thought never even crossed my mind. I was impressed by the Kid's guts for coming in, but was still curious as to what for. I jumped off of the training table and stood in front of him as he approached. I didn't think he was going to try and cheap shot me or anything, but I didn't know what he was going to do, so I played it safe. As he got closer to me a smile overtook his face. He extended a hand towards me.

"Good game man," he said. I know it sounds cliché, but you could have heard a pin drop as everyone waited to see what I was going to do. Sure, he talked a lot of trash out there and even took a couple of good runs at me, but I did the same to him and I was the one who ended up on the winning end, so what the heck was I going to be hacked off about? I grabbed his hand tightly and shook it. He nodded and continued to smile as we shook hands. He looked to be at a loss for words for a moment or two.

"Thanks too," he said.

"For what?"

"For asking me to play." I laughed at the irony of how he got into the game. It was him, after all, who almost stole the prized possession of the whole evening, the bottle of Slivovitz that the guys and I made short work of earlier in the evening.

"Thanks for trying to steal that bottle off of me. If you hadn't done that, I would have never met you," I said. Everyone shared a laugh with that even though most of the guys in the room didn't know the back story to our relationship yet.

"Man, it felt good to be out there, even though we lost."

"I'm glad you enjoyed it...and sorry about scoring that brilliant game-winner." I didn't feel the need to apologize for gloating. It was a great goal and an incredible come-from-behind victory led by a slightly overweight has-been who hadn't felt like he had done something special with his life in a long time. I considered the feat something worth talking about for a very long time and I am sure that most of my new teammates would have agreed with me.

"I have to admit, that was a great goal. I have to admit though man, I didn't think you had it in you," he said.

"I didn't either, but I'm glad I did." I slapped him on the shoulder and we all stood around in an awkward silence for a few moments. I felt a tap on my back and turned to see that Goran was passing a beer across Tomislav's back to me. I knew the beer wasn't meant for me and felt badly that I hadn't extended one earlier. I reached over my shoulder and grabbed it. Even though mine was almost empty, I knew that it would have been a big-time jerk maneuver not to offer it to a worthy foe.

"Hey, why don't you have a beer with us?" The Kid shuffled his feet in front of me and spoke softly when he replied.

"Nah man, I think I'm okay."

"You serious?"

"Yeah man. I'm fine man."

I raised the beer up in front of me and got ready to pop it open.
"Last call."

"It's all you," he said. I popped it and took a hearty chug.

"So what's with the sudden change of heart about the partying?"

"I got to get fit man. I think I'm going to try and play again man," he said as he patted what was still a pretty healthy-looking midsection.

"Play where?"

"You know, for real man. Like with a team and uniforms and all that. Like tonight." The guys around the room didn't know whether to laugh or cry, so they all just stayed quiet.

"Even with a real team you aren't going to get another night like tonight. Most of it is just Sunday kick-arounds. No lights, no locker rooms," I said.

"Hey man, I don't care. I just want to play again. Be apart of something man." The hints were certainly there, but I obviously wasn't catching any of them. I had to admit that I was still pretty caught up in replaying my own accomplishments from the evening to see how much the Kid had actually proven to himself in what was really just a short period of time. Tomislav leaned in to me and I was worried that he was going to tell me that he wasn't feeling well and that he wanted to return to the hospital. Instead he casually whispered what was painfully obvious to everyone in the locker room except me.

"Why don't you ask him to play for your team?" I paused and took a small sip of my beer as I looked around the room. Everyone was looking at me, dumbfounded, wondering how many more hints I was going to force the Kid to drop before asking him a question I honestly didn't know I had the authority to ask. My brother finally stepped in and rescued me from looking like a complete jerk.

"Why don't you play with us?"

"Really?"

"Sure. We could you some speed up front."

167

"I take offense to that comment," I blurted out.

"Relax, you play in the midfield," countered my brother. Everyone laughed.

"Thanks for the offer, but can I think about it first?"

"No," I said firmly.

"Why not?"

"Because we need you and your speed right away," I said. I could tell that if we didn't wrap the Kid up right away, he might fall back into the lifestyle he was living just hours ago and then the probability that we would never see him again would have been pretty high. I was still having a hard time visualizing myself on the same side of the field as him, but it never hurt to have young legs in a lineup. I was also glad that the game had such an impact on him.

"Look at this, one night, two new signings!" My brother yelled out to everyone.

"Now, why don't you two hug and get it over with," chimed Goran. The whole room erupted in cheers. The guys closed in on us again and doused us both with beer this time. The Kid soaked up every minute of it, because even though he lost the game, he had won something that he probably didn't think was ever going to come along in his life...some support. The locker room quickly returned to the noisy chaotic state that it was in when we first got off the field. Everyone was trying to talk over each other, emphasizing their best play of the game over their teammates.

Goran and Sasha went around the room and congratulated each player one at a time and offered them another beer.

Tomislav stood quietly, leaning against the trainer's table, taking it all in. The Kid was talking to me about how fit he was going to get and how hard he was going to work to earn a spot on the team and how excited he was to be a part of it, but it was all going in one ear and out the other as I watched Tomislav watching everyone else. He stood there sipping his beer, a faint smile painted on his face. His eyes were scanning the room, but his head somewhere else.

The door to the locker room opened again and Cowboy Chris popped his head in, only to be met with a chorus of congratulatory toasts from my teammates as they disrobed for the showers.

"Good game ref!" They shouted to him.

"Way to let us play!" Cowboy Chris was amused by the response to his rookie-refereeing and tipped his hat to the guys as he held the door open just enough for him to see what was going on.

"Thanks guys. Just a warning, we have a female intruder." The guys who were disrobed scooted into the showers and the guys who were in the middle of disrobing wrapped towels around themselves or simply put back on their smelly, sweaty articles of clothing. Cowboy Chris worked his way across the room to me and raised an eyebrow at the Kid standing next to me.

"He's our newest signing," I said.

"No joke?"

"Seriously."

"I reckon I might have to buy season tickets to see ya guys play," said Cowboy Chris as he accepted a beer from Goran.

"Very funny," I said, considering the fact that most games we would play from there on out would have fans that could be counted on one hand in attendance. The door to the locker room slowly popped open and in walked Angela. Everyone stopped what they were doing just to check her out. She didn't look as angry as she did earlier in the evening, but she didn't look as excited either. She exchanged polite smiles with the guys as she walked across the room towards her father and me. Goran offered her a beer, but she silently declined with just a wave of her hand. When she finally did reach her dad, her voice was hushed and with the showers running and talk of the victory still running amuck, it was hard for anyone who wasn't within feet of us to discern what was going on. She laid a gentle hand on the sleeve of Tomislav's jacket.

"Hey dad, we need to get going." Tomislav's eyes widened as he was forced to take his mind off his own thoughts and deal with hers.

"Where?"

"Home...where else?" Angela gently stroked her dad's jacket sleeve and I could tell that Tomislav didn't like it, but he wasn't going to make her stop in front of everyone. I could also tell that going home at that moment was not part of his plan. He took a long, deliberate sip of his beer as he tried to stall his very caring, but also very stubborn daughter.

"I don't think I go home now," he said.

"Do you want to go to the hospital?"

"No." Angela took her hand off his sleeve and crossed her arms. The noise in the locker room started to subside as everyone tried to listen in to the conversation.

"Then what do you want to do dad? You need to get some rest."

"We must go out and celebrate the game."

170

"Dad, you're in no condition to go out." He placed a comforting hand on her cheek.

"Angela, I love you very much. But I am too old for you to tell me that I can't go out."

"But–"

"That was great soccer game out there and now we must go out to talk more about it and drink and eat. That is why we play the game in the first place," he said.

"Tomislav, maybe you should head home for some rest," I said and immediately regretted it. Tomislav didn't even shoot me a look, he just completely ignored me. He knew me better than to think that I truly meant it. Sasha looked too tired to fight his brother on it and Goran, not surprisingly, was all for it.

"Where do we go Tomislav?"
"Cigo's."

"I'll go get my car," said Goran.

"But you don't drive."

"You're right."

"You never drove."

"I never had license."

"Why not?"

"Because you did," quipped Goran. We all shared a laugh while everyone tried to figure out in their heads what was going to happen next. Angela shot me a look that begged for help. I was ready to let her get pissed at me, but not about to be responsible for souring Tomislav's night.

"I can drive," said Cowboy Chris.

"Me too," offered my brother.

"S-s-somebody can p-p-pile on my scooter with me," said Sasha to some laughs.

"We'll have to jump in with somebody, we walked," I said. Tomislav stood there, shaking his head.

"We walk. We all walk," he demanded. Angela let out a dramatic sigh of defeat, but nobody even questioned him. And with that, Tomislav went over to the cooler, grabbed a new beer, popped it and walked out the locker room door and into the cold, foggy, night.

CHAPTER 23

There couldn't have been a more eclectic mix of pedestrians strolling around town through the wind, fog and sporadic rain than the motley crew we had assembled to venture down to Cigo's for our post-game celebration. Surprisingly, it was Tomislav, Goran and Sasha, who was walking with his scooter, who led the way as the rest of us tagged closely behind. The awful weather didn't seem to faze the old guys at all as they relentlessly continued their overlapping conversations with every step. My brother and Mr. Nowinski were flanked by a handful of players from my team and the young guys who had decided to tag along. Mr. Nowinski encouraged the young guys from the Rec Center to come along with promises that the meals were going to be taken care of by someone. Who that was going to be was anyone's guess. I knew it wasn't going to be me, so it was something I decided not to worry about. The Kid had somehow positioned himself next to Angela on the sidewalk and was in her ear about his upcoming "official" comeback.

Angela had always been able to exercise extreme patience when she chose to, and on this occasion, she chose to as she let the Kid go on and on about how much of an impact he was going to have on his new team, my team. I walked next to Cowboy Chris who was still caught up in how hot Angela looked and seemed to have already forgotten what a great game I had just played. "She's so smokin' hot pardner," he kept repeating as he looked over his shoulder to see her walking alongside the Kid.

173

"Why don't you just ask her out then?"

"I couldn't do that, you'd get pissed pardner."

"No I wouldn't. She'd tell you no anyway."

"Ya think so?"

"I know so...watch," I said. I was feeling pretty spry and turned to Angela who was in mid-listen with the Kid. I didn't feel bad interrupting.

"Hey, Angela...would you ever go out with Chris?" Without hesitation she replied coldly.

"No." I turned to Cowboy Chris and gently patted his shoulder.

"She never dated anyone from town."

"She dated you!"

"We actually never technically dated I don't think."

"Then what were ya guys doin' all those years?" I turned around to see her staring at me. She ignored the Kid and had both her ears fully focused on our conversation, because it was a topic even she was curious about and one that she and I never did really have the chance to address.

"We were just having a good time, trying to figure out for ourselves what we were doing. Unfortunately, we both took too long to figure it out and ended up going our own separate ways," I said.

"If you ask me, that was the dumbest decision of your whole life pardner," said Cowboy Chris loud enough so that maybe Angela would hear that he was on her side.

"I would tend to agree with you on that Chris." I didn't even turn around to see if Angela had heard the last part, it would have been too cheesy to see her reaction to something her and I should have talked about years ago and saved ourselves a lot of heartache and pain. I raced up to my brother and patted his back.

"Could I borrow your cell phone?"

"Sure. How's that tux treating you?"

"Great, thanks for letting me borrow it," I said in a sarcastic tone.

"You know, if you hook up with Angela it's all because of the tux."

"Whatever," I replied with a laugh. I took his cell and purposefully let myself drift to the back of the pedestrian caravan. As I drifted past Angela though, she corralled me by the shirt collar.

"Are you talking behind my back?"

"You wish."

"Are you going to rescue me from Baby Beckham or what?"

"Not yet, it's too much fun watching him hit on you."

"He's not hitting on me, he's just being nice!"

"Sure he is."

The Kid continued to talk through our entire conversation. He wasn't pissed about being interrupted by me at all, but wasn't about to stop talking either. He continued his conversation with Mr. Nowinski, who had ended up beside him somehow and reluctantly lent him a kind ear. Angela tried to continue our conversation now that we were sort of alone, but I had to make a phone call and I had to make it quickly. She continued on about something as I let myself drift back away from the pack and away from her.

"Where are you going?"

"I've got to make a call," I said, offering up the phone as proof. She let the group get ahead of her and then she stopped in her tracks.

She crossed her arms and shot a dirty, cold, hard look at me as I tried to dial the phone. I hung up.

"What?"

"You know, it wasn't too long ago that the most important thing on your mind was calling the girls after games," she said.

"How can you still remember that? It was so long ago," I said.

"I remember, because I always wanted to go with you, but there was always someone else you had your eyes set on," she said. I would have loved to have continued the argument with her, because at least it was a form of conversation. It was something I had missed for a very long time, but I had to make a call.

"Could we continue this at Cigo's, I've really got to make this call," I pleaded. She didn't even reply and instead turned in a huff and stormed back into the group and eventually ended up back with the Kid where she draped an arm around his shoulder. It was a cruel attempt at making me jealous. I was left to make my call and caught some curious stares from members of our pedestrian posse. I made the call, which only took a few moments and then quickly caught up to the group that was a half-block ahead of me. My brother seemed upset by the secretive conversation.

"Who was that?"

"Don't worry about it. It's not like I'm going to go sign with somebody else or something," I said.

"We've got the Kid now, I don't even know if we need you anymore," he shot back to a handful of snickers from our teammates.

"You might not need me? Then maybe I should retire."

"Let's not get hasty now Niko," said Mr. Nowinski.

"Could I get my phone back?"

"You need it now?"

"Yeah, I've got my own secret phone call to make."

I had to give the guys in front credit; they wanted to celebrate and were getting all of us there a lot quicker than I would have thought with an obviously obsessed Tomislav leading the charge sans cane or any other method of assistance. He was still unleashing some nasty coughs from time to time, but otherwise seemed to be holding up pretty well. My legs and back ached and all I wanted to do was sit down and eat and relax for a while, but I also knew that my body could and would operate on the plenty of adrenaline it had stored up if it had to. And I was expecting that it was going to have to. Angela's attempt at making me jealous was short-lived. She left the Kid and moved to the front to hang with her dad and the guys. She curled her arm through her dad's as he escorted her through century-old neighborhoods to the oldest restaurant in town.

I worked my way up through the group as we crossed through the parking lot and toward the front door of the restaurant as the rain subsided. I received pats on the shoulder from everyone except Angela, who kicked me in the butt, and not in a loving way, as I passed her. Cowboy Chris handed me a cold beer from the little cooler he had carried down with him to keep us all replenished during our walk.

I grabbed the door first and started to let everyone in. I could tell that Cigo's hadn't changed a bit; it was just as crowded and loud and as I had remembered it from many years ago.

The food came in huge portions and the drinks were poured heavy. Conversations were yelled, not spoken and the bartender and waitresses were always short with their words and gracious with their actions.

Tomislav and the guys smacked my cheek affectionately as they passed by me and into the madness that was going to play host to our post-game celebration. Angela actually pecked me on the cheek and my brother mimicked her by doing the same, much to the delight of our teammates. I started to seriously question whether signing with them was the right choice, not for their lack of playing ability, but simply due to the fact that most of them actually thought that my brother was funny. Mr. Nowinski wheeled by me and delivered a right-handed karate chop across my gut.

"Are you buying tonight."

"No, but somebody hopefully will."

"The kids don't have money for this, and neither do I."

"Don't worry about it, it'll get taken care of," I offered confidently, though I had no clue how it was all going to get taken care of. Everything else had been taking care of itself and I figured it was time to relax and little bit and let things play out. I figured that maybe if they asked me to kick in for the tab at the end of the night that I could extort my brother to pay otherwise I wouldn't play for his team or coach his high school team. But that wouldn't have been right. As everyone was making their way to the bar, I caught up with Tomislav to see how he was doing.

"How are you feeling?" I could tell that the walk had taken its toll on him. "I'll be okay Peter. Stop worrying about me," he said in an annoyed voice.

"Let me know if you need anything," I said. Tomislav grabbed me by the shoulder and summoned a bit of energy to hold on tightly for a moment.

"I need you to leave me alone and let me have a good time and you have a good time too, okay?" He mustered a faint smile, but I could tell that he was fading.

"Okay, I'll leave you alone and I'll have a good time."

"Good. Let's celebrate," he said as Goran passed us shots of something that's color I couldn't necessarily define.

"Hey Goran, I'm sorry, but I don't have any cash," I said apologetically.

"The MVP never pay for his own drinks."

"Thanks." Goran sidled up to me as we held the mystery shots in our hands. He placed a firm arm around my neck.

"You play the game tonight the way it is supposed to be played...with this!" He pounded his fist against his chest.

"I love watching you play Niko!" he added as he slammed his shot effortlessly.

"Thanks Goran. But I'll be honest with you...I'm pretty wiped out right now. That game did a number on me."

"No, no Niko. It's no time for rest now. We are just getting started," he insisted. I was afraid of what Goran just said. The old guys always seemed to be able to summon the energy to party well into the night after games, especially good games where things went their way. I was waiting for my second, or I guess it would have been third or even fourth wind to kick in, but it wasn't happening.

"Niko, get drink in you, it's good for the blood. It will give you energy," he said. I admired Goran's relentless pursuit of a good time and he was right.

179

It was no time to get soft or to be tired. He slapped me hard on the back and snapped up another shot off the bar.

"I be back," is all he said before he disappeared into the crowd in order to follow what looked to be a pretty good-looking waitress. I grabbed an empty stool and sat patiently at the bar waiting for the bartender to ask for my order. I scanned the room for Angela, but couldn't see her. Then suddenly, I was bumped off my stool, a hit that sent me sprawling to the floor. I jumped up ready for action, only to be met by an obviously drunk and upset Cowboy Chris.

"I reckon I'm just not good enough to get the news straight from you anymore," he said with more disappointment than anger in his voice.

"What are you talking about?" He took a mighty slug of his beer before he continued on.

"Why didn't ya tell me you're the new high school coach?"

"I didn't think it was a big deal."

"Well, it is. Everyone's talkin' about it pardner."

"Yeah, right," I said. Cowboy Chris got up in my face for emphasis. I could tell that he really was upset that he just found out even though I couldn't figure out why.

"I'm serious pardner, all those kids that played tonight are talkin' about how they want to come out for the team next year. They want to talk to ya, but they're scared. I reckon that after seeing ya play tonight, I don't blame them. Ya were an animal out there pardner."

With that, Cowboy Chris lightened his mood and backhanded me across the chest. It hurt and I was getting tired of everyone hitting me, but I wasn't about to do anything about it. Mr. Nowinski wheeled towards us with a few of the young guys in tow.

"I was telling the boys how important it is to keep those grades up if they plan on playing for you next season. Isn't that right coach?" When I heard Mr. Nowinski call me coach it freaked me out. I was going to be a role model for a lot of kids from here on out and it was something I wasn't used to. But I knew that I had it in me to get it done and all the events of the night had helped me prove to myself that I could accomplish something if I really applied myself.

"You guys have got to keep those grades up. School first...then soccer," I said. Mr. Nowinski nodded enthusiastically as I am sure it is a philosophy he had been preaching to the guys for years.

"You hear that guys? No grades, no soccer! Right from the coach's mouth," he asserted. The guys nodded and smiled. They looked excited about the prospects of playing next year. Xavier was amongst the group and had the biggest smile on his face.

"You guys all plan on coming out?"

"They'll be there coach. You just tell them where and when," Mr. Nowinski said on behalf of them all.

"In the meantime, hit the books, but don't forget to keep playing too," I said. They all smiled and came by and shook my hand one by one. They all thanked me for getting them in the game and also for taking the coaching job. They all called me coach.

It all felt good, really good, but I was nervous. Making commitments hadn't been one of my strong suits and in one night I had made quite a few, but I was living up to them and feeling much better about myself than I had in years. Cowboy Chris handed me another shot. This time the color of it was too familiar to mistake.

"Jaeger?"

"Ya better believe it pardner." We both shot it without chasers and shook our heads in unison to absorb the hearty taste.

"Ya excited to be coachin'?"

"Sure, I'm just glad to have the chance to have an impact on someone. To be able to maybe make a difference, you know? Some of those kids out there tonight could really play. It would be cool if one or a few of them went on to play college ball or even pro one day. Even if they don't end up playing at a higher level, if their experience playing for me has a positive impact on their lives...that would be cool. To know that I've done something good."

"I reckon that ya must be blind if ya don't realize how much of an impact you've had on somebody," he said. The Kid walked up to us with a bottle of water in his hand.

"So, are you going to ask me to be your assistant or are you going to make me beg man?" His comments caught me off-guard, but they appeared to be a bit rehearsed. It was something that I think that Cowboy Chris had something to do with. I shot him a nasty stare. He shrugged his shoulders.

"You already heard too, huh?"

"It's all over town man."

"All over town? It happened like two hours ago," I said.

"Everyone's excited about it. I think that you and me would make a great coaching team man. We could bring a championship home man! You

think I could coach with you next season?" He shuffled from side to side and took a handful of nervous sips from his water bottle. I was impressed that he got it all out without even an ounce of alcohol in him. He sounded serious too, but I knew that this was just the beginning. I also knew that everyone had to start somewhere, sometimes more than once.

"You think you can stay out of trouble?" I asked him squarely.

"Definitely man. I'm outta all that crap man."

"Can you stay clean? We can't have you around the young guys if you're drinking or any of that other stuff." He held up the water bottle and smiled.

"This is it for me from now on man. I'm gonna be playing and coaching with you, I won't have time for anymore of that crap man," he assured me. I knew he had a point and I knew it was my responsibility to help give him an opportunity. I looked him up and down and he looked way better than he did just a few hours ago. He had showered and cleaned up pretty nice. I stood up from my barstool and extended a hand to him.

"Welcome to the team, coach," I said. He grabbed my hand and pulled me in for a great, big hug. It felt awkward, but I didn't blame the Kid for his unbridled affection. He let go of me and pulled back.

"Sorry," he said.

"Don't worry about it. Now go have some fun. But stay away from Angela. She's too old for you." I wagged a firm finger at him that was knocked down by none other than Angela herself.

"You're calling me old now?"

"I guess I am."

"You're just full of compliments, aren't you?" I didn't answer her because out of the corner of my eye I noticed a large man in a dark suit who had just entered the room. I wanted to find my brother and kick his butt in front of everyone for inviting him. Angela could see the anger in my face. She turned and saw him hanging his coat.

"Didn't you see him at the game?"

"I did, but I didn't think he'd show up here. Frank must have told him."

"What are you going to do?"

"What should I do?" Even though we gone through some rocky times, Angela had given me good advice as a friend and had been there in many of my times of need after my mom died, so I valued her thoughts. Plus, she was never afraid to be honest with me. In fact, we were always pretty brutally honest with each other. I stood there and watched him hang his coat and then straighten out his tie. He ran his hands through his dyed, greased-back hair and took a long look around the room. My brother must have been in the bathroom or something, because he would have been the first one to run up to my dad. Unfortunately, our eyes met and he slowly started walking towards us. Angela braced herself for the worst.

"Do you want me to stay here with you?"

"Yeah," I said without hesitation.

He scanned the room looking for other familiar faces, but there were none. He was too good and too sophisticated for a real group of people having real fun. It wasn't one of his over-priced and overrated lawyer hangouts where the waiters relentlessly hawked over you expecting their thirty percent tips. An obviously drunk local went to get up from his seat and bumped him. Instead of getting all fired up at the man, my dad laughed and patted the guy on the back. It surprised me to see a slightly human and forgiving side to him. As he got closer to me I could see a kindness in his face that I hadn't seen in many years. He recognized Angela instantly.

"Hello Angela."

"Hi Mr. Casey," she replied. There was a silence before he said anything to me, because I think he had a few things that he wanted to get out first. But he was a bright man and he knew that only one thing could open the conversation.

"That was a heck of a game you played tonight son," he said. I didn't know how to reply at first, because he caught me off-guard with something positive right out of the gates. It always used to be questions about why I couldn't do better or why I couldn't just give up on my dreams to become a big, hotshot lawyer like he was. It was always questions about when I was going to figure out what the heck I was going to do with my life and when I was going to get married and start a family and live by the formula that he had lived by for so long and apparently had done him so much good.

"Thanks dad," I said.

"Your brother told me that you took the coaching job at the high school."

"Yeah, we'll see what happens."

"Are you going to try and teach too?"

"Maybe, I haven't really given that much thought yet. I still have quite a bit of work left on the house."

"Have you put the roof on it yet?" I couldn't help but laugh.

"Not yet dad, but soon," I promised him. There was an awkward silence as we both tried to figure out what to do next. I appreciated my dad giving me the house to live in and work on, but since my mom died, I felt like there had always been something missing in our family. I felt like I kept looking for it, whereas my dad and brother simply moved on. I always resented them for it. My brother finally made his way over to us and I politely excused myself to go find Tomislav and the guys. My dad and I were caught up and tomorrow would bring with it a new chance to rekindle the relationship. But for now, there were other more pressing things on my mind, like how much longer Tomislav had left. I left on a search for the guys. Angela joined me in the hunt. We worked our way through the throngs of locals who inhabited the bar and into the restaurant area, which had been emptying, since it was getting late.

The Kid, Tomislav, Goran, Sasha and Mr. Nowinski were all seated at a table on the edge of what was a small, parquet dance floor. Players from both teams were littered around neighboring tables. A two-man-band made up of gray-haired twins played songs from the old country on a small stage using a sound system that had clearly (no pun intended) heard better days. Angela and I were simultaneously flagged down by the guys as we entered the room.

Everyone had a drink in their hand that they motioned us over with, except the Kid, who proudly displayed his water bottle to me as he waved us over. He optimistically pulled out a chair for Angela as she approached the table. She thanked him politely and took her own chair between her dad and Goran.

I sat down next to Mr. Nowinski and an empty chair. The guys, namely Goran, were in the middle of an obviously entertaining story which had Sasha near tears...the good kind of tears.

"And then Tomislav hit him in his chest and knock the guy on his butt," roared Goran.

"I r-r-remember that," said Sasha. I couldn't pick up what it was, but I wanted to know the gist of what was making everyone so happy. It was good to see everyone laughing so hard.

"What're you guys laughing about?"

"Do you remember when Tomislav fight the guy in front of stadium?"

"Sure...I broke it up," I said.

"I b-b-broke it up," argued Sasha.

"I think a lot of us had to break it up. Tomislav was so pissed that he wouldn't stop going after the poor guy," I said.

"You remember why Tomislav fight the guy?"

"No," I said.

"It was because the guy ask Rose out on date twenty years earlier," said Goran who was on the verge of tears because he was laughing so hard. On second thought, I did remember. Tomislav was pissed that the guy showed up out of the blue to watch a game.

When Tomislav realized it was the same guy who asked his wife out on a date at a dance twenty years earlier, Tomislav went after him before the guy even set foot in the stadium. The guy didn't get the chance to watch any soccer that day, or any other day after that, at Daniel's Field.

187

"The good old days, huh Tomislav," I said. He smiled and toasted me with his drink. He still had a little sparkle in his eyes, but it looked like he was forcing it. He appeared to be battling his body which looked like it was more ready to lie down than party on. I didn't blame him at all, in fact, it surprised me that he made it this far. I just hoped that he had a little more time left in him. Goran took back control of the table.

"Niko, you were in lot of fights, yes?"

"Yes."

"And you win a lot of fights, yes?"

"No," I answered honesty. Everyone erupted in laughter. I did have more than my fair share of fights and took my fair share of lumps, just like all the tough guys at Daniel's Field did over the years. None of us left there better looking than when we arrived. The Kid couldn't contain his enthusiasm for the spirited conversation. He chimed in with a question of his own that I wished he would have just kept to himself.

"Is that how you messed up your hand?"

"What?" I said.

"Not you man...Tomislav. Is that how you messed up your hand man?" The table instantly fell silent. I had no clue how Tomislav was going to handle it. He took his right hand, which had been on the table next to his drink, and slid it under the table.

What seemed like hours passed. I didn't even think Tomislav was going to answer and it was too quiet and we were all too close to each other for me to whisper to the Kid to strike his question from the record.

"No, it was not a fight," said Tomislav. He pulled his curled up right hand back up from his lap and inspected it.

I know the Kid was just trying to be inquisitive and keep some conversation going, but he was really just buzz-killed the entire night. I had heard that Tomislav got it caught in the nets while he was fishing and that it tore up the palm of his hand so badly that it rendered it useless. Tomislav was so embarrassed that he let it happen to himself that he got out of fishing shortly after that and sold his entire fleet. Ever since then, he just kept it balled up so nobody could see it. I didn't know if I could even attempt to change the subject and definitely didn't want to interrupt Tomislav if he was going to continue on.

"I'm going outside to smoke," he said.

"You can smoke in here," said Goran.

"I'll be outside," said Tomislav firmly. He slowly got up from the table and made his way out the back of the restaurant and into the alley.

"He shouldn't be alone," said Angela.

"Do you want me to go out there with him?"

"Yeah, Niko. Go with him," she ordered. Before I left the stone cold quiet table, I tried to loosen the mood again.

"Sasha, why don't you go sing with the guys?" He stared back at me in apparent shock.

"I o-o-only sing at ch-ch-church."

"So why not sing here?"

"B-b-because they can throw th-things at you h-h-here, they can't at ch-ch, church," he countered. A faint laugh rose from the table.

"When I get back, I expect to see you singing." Angela could tell that I was trying to bring the triumphant mood back to the evening and then helped out in my cause to get him to sing.

"Come on Uncle Sasha, mom said that you've been singing beautifully in church."

"I have," he said in a fleeting moment of self-confidence.

"So go up there and try it? Come on, we're all friends."

"W-w-will you go see if it's o-o-okay with the guys in the b-b-band?"

"Sure...I'll be right back. Better start warming up your voice in the meantime," she said as she left for the stage.

CHAPTER 24

The trash-strewn, car-wide alley probably wasn't the safest place in the world to hang out and have a chat, but with the way the whole night had gone down, getting mugged was the last thing on my mind. Tomislav was half-finished with a cigarette and paced the narrow width of the alley furiously.

"Tomislav, you okay?"

"Too many mistakes Niko," he said.

"What are you talking about Tomislav?" He took a healthy drag of his cigarette then spiked it into the ground.

"I made too many mistakes Niko. My hand...so stupid!"

"We all make mistakes Tomislav. You've just got to figure out a way to move on."

"And with Angela...more mistakes!"

"Like what?"

"I was always too hard on her. She's such a beautiful woman, I should have been more gentle with her."

"You did the best you could Tomislav."

"No I didn't. I should have been more gentle. Then maybe, she wouldn't have left," he said. I walked over to him and laid a comforting hand on his shoulder. I thought about how he had come to this country with his family and went to work as a teenager for the next fifty years of his life with hardly a break except for those Sunday afternoon games and a couple of late night training sessions.

I remembered him telling me how he worked two jobs to help support his mom and dad and pay for special schools to help his brother with his speech problem and then continued the workaholic trend when he married Rose and started his own family.

I thought about how he used to tell me that a career as a pro soccer player wasn't even in the cards for him even though he definitely had the talent because playing soccer for a living wasn't even an option back in the day. So all he did was work. And play some soccer when then opportunity presented itself, which it did, at least for a few years. Nobody could blame him for being hard. It's all he knew. That's how he got himself and his family through life. Being gentle or soft was never an option for him, so I didn't blame him for not knowing how to help Angela deal with his sickness and the possibility of growing old without one of her parents. I guided him over to an old, unsteady-looking chair that look like it was used by the waiters and waitresses on their smoke breaks. I knew that because in the rickety chair sat an old aluminum ashtray overstuffed with cigarette butts. He slowly sat down in it and pulled a cigarette from his own jacket pocket. I extended my hand for him to give me one.

"Niko, you don't smoke."

"Tonight is special, just one with you." He smiled and obliged me with the last one he had in his pack. He lit his and then I leaned in to him and he lit mine.

"Listen Tomislav, Angela stayed away because she wanted to be with that guy. It had nothing to do with you." I didn't want him to feel like his sickness kept her away from home.

"That guy had no business with her," he said emphatically.

"You're right. But the important thing now is that Angela is back. And the main reason she came back is you."

"I love her so much, she's so beautiful." He shook his head and started to cry just a little bit.

"She knows you love her Tomislav," I said confidently.

"Does she?"

"I think so, but it never hurts to let them know."

"I just want her to be happy," he said through a puff of smoke.

"I know you do, and she will be," I said as I tried to inconspicuously wipe a tear from my eye. He snuffed out his cigarette, stood up and laid a firm hand on my shoulder. He looked me square in my eyes with his tired, drooping eyes. A smile came across his face as the tears dried up on his gaunt cheeks.

"Will you take good care of her Niko?"

"Of course I will."

"Forever?" He inquired as he raised a brow. I knew that he didn't just want me to be his daughter's buddy for the rest of our lives. I knew that he was asking me if I was going to marry his daughter.

If I knew that it would be okay with Angela, I would have done it the minute we went back into the restaurant. But there were more pressing issues to be dealt with what was left of the night. I did want to put his mind at ease and be able to assure him somehow that Angela would be alright. After all, his beautiful daughter had been having a pretty rough go of things lately.

193

"Yes, I'll take care of her forever...if she'll let me." He laughed at the last bit of my comment.

"She will let you Niko. I'll put in a good word for you."

"That would be nice." He patted my cheek and walked out into the alley. He spotted a rotted onion lying on the ground and took a couple of steps towards it. He struck it cleanly with his patented left foot and sent it skipping down the alley and towards the main road. He spun around at me with raised eyebrows.

"The lungs may go...but never the touch. You never lose the touch."

"Apparently not."

"Let's go inside and enjoy drink Niko," he demanded. He patted my back and tried to guide me back into the restaurant, but I felt like I needed a few minutes to myself again. For a moment I wondered if I should tell him what he was going through, so that he'd know that tonight might be the last chance for him to tell Angela that he missed her and that he wished he had been more gentle with her and all the things he had told me he wished he had told Angela. But then I decided that it wasn't my place to tell him what was happening with his life. Things were going smoothly and I felt like if he thought it was something important to do, he would do it.

If not, he'd wait and maybe never have the chance to say it, but I knew I couldn't meddle with it. I almost asked him if he knew what was going on, if he knew why or how he was suddenly able to get up after having been bedridden for so long. But I thought otherwise. What was it going to change, except the timing of some last minute words that were maybe, or maybe not, going to be muttered anyway?

The Gift of Stoppage Time

"You go ahead Tomislav, I'll finish my cigarette and be in shortly." He shrugged his shoulders and smiled at me and then went inside. I was curious if he was going to tell Angela what he regretted, but I knew that I couldn't tell him when or how to do it, because this was his time, not mine. He was gone for a few minutes before the back door to the restaurant swung open. I expected to see him again, but it was Angela. She looked happy, which was nice to see. She frowned when she saw the cigarette in my hand though.

"Nice habit," she said wryly.

"It's a novelty, not a habit." She strolled past me and into the middle of the alley.

"I'm sorry for everything...you know," she said softly.

"You don't need to be sorry Angela." She came over to me and plucked the cigarette out of my mouth. Instead of throwing it on the ground and snuffing it out, she took a seductive drag from it.

"I misjudged you. It's kind of funny how that happened, huh? I mean, for as long as I've known you, I've always known you to try and do good things." She slowly extended the cigarette back towards me and slid it into my mouth. I was ashamed at myself for thinking that we were having such an intimate moment at a time like this. She sat down in the chair.

"It's no big deal. Sometimes we just hurt so much that we forget what they're going through. I mean, your dad is the one who's struggling, not us. But it hurts so much to think of them leaving, that it makes it tough to put their suffering into perspective because it's overshadowed by our own pain."

"I know, it's all so crazy...so painful."

"I think the hardest thing to realize is that they're not just leaving us, but they're leaving all of this."

195

"This?"

"Yeah...life. What else is there? I think that the best we can do is help them enjoy this last bit of time that they've been gifted. I don't know how it happens, I just know that it's given to them for a reason and that reason is to enjoy all of the beauty that surrounds them." There was a long pause as Angela fought to contain her emotions.

"But I don't want him to go," she said through a trickle of tears.

"None of us do. It's probably going to hurt for a long time, but in your heart you'll know that you did the right thing and that your dad was happy to have you with him for this night." I knelt down on one knee next to her and laid a comforting hand on her arm.

"You know how a lot of people say that you can't take it with you?"

"Yeah."

"Well, I disagree. I think that you can take it with you and what your dad will take with him is this night and the time he spent with you."

"You think it's that important to him?"

"Absolutely Angela. Do you know how much he loves you?"

"No."

"Well...it's a lot. You're all he ever talks about."

"You mean after work and soccer."

"No, come on! Those things don't even come close when it comes to his love for you."

"That's refreshing to hear, because it never felt that way," she said. I took my hand off her arm and stood up.

"You know Angela, I think that ultimately, when people get ready to leave us, all they really want to know is that their loved ones are going to be okay after they're gone."

"Am I?"

"Are you what?"

"Going to be okay?"

"Yeah, you are. Because I'm going to take good care of you," I said.

"You promise?"

"Yeah, I promise." Angela stood up, stepped towards me and then delivered a playful, back-handed blow to my chest.

"You better, or my dad will kick your ass!"

"I know he will." I grabbed her hand and pulled her into me for a kiss. There was no pulling back or holding back. It was a beautiful kiss that lasted minutes and felt better than the goal I had scored earlier in the evening. We pulled apart and she smiled.

"So, are we finally together?" I didn't want to mince words or make light of anything, so I gave her the answer in the simplest terms that I knew.

"Yes Angela, we're together."

"So what do we do now?"

"I think you help me finish the house."

"What!?"

"Didn't you want to be an interior designer or something?"

"Nice try. I wanted to be a psychologist," she said.

"That's close, isn't it?"

"No."

"How about you help me finish the house and then you can be somebody's wife?"

"Really?"

"Yeah?"

"When?"

"Whenever you want," I said.

"Soon, but not too soon," she said.

"That's fine."

"Really?"

"Yes."

"Is this what you want?"

"It's you that I want. That's all I ever wanted." I tried to back-track and figure out if what I just did was ask her to marry me. I didn't think for a minute to ask her for clarification. She grabbed my hand and we charged back into the party, her smiling and my heart beating a hundred miles an hour. Once we were back inside, I was met with a handful of curious and slightly annoyed stares from the guys, who were all seated around the table on the edge of the dance floor.

We made our way back over to them, Angela clutching my hand tightly the whole way over. The guys quickly caught on to the hand-holding and each did their own version of a startled double-take. I didn't know what kind of crap I was going to have to put up with from them, but I was ready for anything. The dining area had gotten packed with second-shift working longshoremen who came in for their 10 pm "lunch" break. New life had been breathed into the place as Sasha belted out oldies tunes with the help of the twin brothers while the rest of us sang along.

Cowboy Chris table-hopped from one to another, chatting up all the different groups of guys he knew from his many years spent in town and on the docks. Much to my surprise, there wasn't a hint of stutter in Sasha's singing. He did have a beautiful voice and seemed to be enjoying every bit of his live performance. The guys at the table sang and clapped along as the night grew older and older. Angela let go of my hand and sat next to her dad in the only seat available near him. I took a seat opposite her and next to my brother.

"Where's dad?"

"He left," said my brother.

"Why?"

"He said he had to be up early for work tomorrow."

"Sure he does," I said sarcastically. I knew that my dad had done what he came to do. It was good to see him show an interest in my life again. I knew that things weren't going to be patched up overnight. But it was a start.

I watched Tomislav across the table. He had his arm draped over Angela's shoulder again. His face looked really drawn and he looked tired, very tired. I knew that time was running out, whether any of us wanted to believe it or not. There was still something I needed to happen to complete the night and there was no way for me to know when it would happen, until it happened.

I sat back in my seat and tried to enjoy my drink. I looked around the table and saw Goran playfully arguing with the Kid about something.

My brother sat next to me in a fatigue-induced state watching Sasha sing. I could overhear Cowboy Chris working the room with his buddies, telling them all about the great game that they had missed at Daniel's Field.

199

Some cared and some didn't, but Cowboy Chris didn't care. He told stories from the game to whoever would let him sit at their table for a minute or two. Mr. Nowinski was sitting with the players from the Rec Center that he had sent over and they looked to be having a great time rehashing the evenings' events, even though they were on the losing end. Angela sat across from me holding her dad's bad hand on the table, watching her Uncle sing and watching me take it all in. She wouldn't stop smiling and it made me happy and sad all at the same time to know that her emotions were going to be on another involuntary roller coaster ride sometime very soon.

The stern-looking bartender with the permanently furrowed mono-brow came over to our table and I thought for a moment that we might be getting kicked out. Instead, she tapped me on the shoulder and waved for me to follow her. There was no way I was going to disobey her order. She guided me over to the bar and then leaned in to me and whispered something too confidential to blurt out loud.

"There is a lady out front asking for you," she said. I knew immediately who it was, but was suddenly at a loss for how I was going to make all this happen at this time in the night.

"Thanks," I said as I stood by the bar motionless. A thousand thoughts ran sprints through my mind as I looked over at our table that was still in a celebratory mood.

I quickly walked up to Sasha who was in between songs. He had just taken a mammoth chug of bottled water and was wiping away a flood of sweat off his billboard-sized forehead with a napkin. I stretched up towards him on the small, slightly-raised stage and he leaned down over me. I felt dozens of drops of his warm sweat pour all over my head. I shook it off, because

The Gift of Stoppage Time

despite the fact that it was extremely gross, it was unimportant for the moment. I whispered in his ear what was going on. He pulled back from me and nodded emphatically in agreement. I wished that he had done it with more subtlety, but Sasha wasn't known for being a quick thinker and was too massive of a man to do anything without people noticing. He started up on another song as I walked away from the stage and towards the front door. I stole a quick glance over at our table and could see Angela shooting an inquisitive stare my way. I gave her a nod and a smile and she returned the gesture.

I reached the door and slowly opened it. Out in front of the restaurant, in a beautiful dress that lacked imagination but exemplified class, was Rose. She wore little make up and had her hair up in a tightly wound bun. A shawl sheltered her shoulders from the night's biting air. She lifted her head when I came out and greeted me with a nervous smile as she clutched her purse tightly in front of her.

"I don't think I can do this Niko," she said. I tried to get her to relax.

"You look very beautiful Rose."

"Thank you Niko. But I don't know about this."

"About what?"

"How many people are in there?" I knew it was bad to lie and I didn't want to, but I didn't know what else to do. There was no way that Rose was going to waltz in there with dozens of strange eyes cast upon her. In recent years, she rarely left the house, let alone parade through a restaurant in her Sunday clothes in front of what she thought might be dozens of critical stares. It was imperative that I got her in there though. The whole night had come so far, we had all had so much fun, that this truly was the icing on the cake.

Even though Tomislav and Rose rarely ventured out together, I knew he would like it, because everything was different on this night. I wanted to persuade Rose to come in, but I also didn't want to press her on it. She was a grown woman and the last thing I wanted to do was make her uncomfortable. She would have had a hard time forgiving me for that. And I didn't need anything more in my life to regret. I decided to be honest and hoped that she would come around.

"There are quite a few people in there, Rose, I'm not going to lie to you." She clutched her purse even tighter and for a brief moment it looked like she was going to spin around and jump right back into the taxi cab that sat idling at the curb just feet behind her.

"Hundreds?"

"No...a few dozen." I knew that the number might scare her off and didn't actually know how accurate it was.

But I knew that if she thought there were only a few people in there and then she walked in and saw a couple hundred eyes staring at her, it might have been her health that we would be worrying about instead of Tomislav's.

"Is Angela in there?"

"Everyone is in there Rose. Come on, it'll be fine. You'll all be together. Tomislav will love it. You'll love it." I extended my arm for her to grab a hold of. She turned away from me and stared at the cab for what felt like minutes. I knew that I couldn't push any harder. It was her choice to make. This was the final piece of the puzzle for the night and if it didn't work out, despite what had already been accomplished, I probably would have felt some failure. She started taking steps towards the cab. The driver jumped out and opened the back door for her.

The Gift of Stoppage Time

Instinctively, I went after her. Before she could duck into the cab, I gently touched her arm. She turned to me with tears in her eyes.

"I don't want him to go Niko." I slowly pulled her in to me and nodded for the cab driver to take off, which he did.

"Tomislav is such a good man," she wailed through tears. "I don't know what I will do without him." Their relationship spanned half a century and I figured that it was going to be harder for her, more than anybody, to get used to life without him. I didn't know what to say to help ease her pain. I gently pulled myself away from her and handed her the handkerchief that was stuffed into my pocket. She wiped tears from her eyes and then blew her nose something fierce into it. Then she handed it back to me. I took it back purely out of respect.

"How does he look?"

"He looks pretty good."

"He's a good-looking man," she said.

"Yes he is," I said somewhat uncomfortably. I extended my arm to her again.

"Will you join us?" She looked back over her shoulder at the empty curb. The cab was long gone. She looped her arm through mine and wiped away a few lingering tears with the corner of her shawl. I took a deep breath before I opened the door and then heard her do the same.

CHAPTER 25

I opened the door and was unceremoniously bumped by a couple of guys on their way back to work. I shielded Rose from them and then held the door open for her as I guided her inside. I could tell that she was shocked by how many people were still there, because it was late. But I think that my warnings helped curb her fears just a bit. We started to slowly make our way into the restaurant unnoticed until the music stopped suddenly and Sasha joyfully announced our entrance.

"Exexex-cuse-me-evv...evv..everbody. I wu...would like ttt...to...int...introduce RRRR...Rose!" Everyone in the restaurant surprisingly went silent and directed their attention our way. I was even paralyzed for a moment by all the attention. Luckily for me, Rose had already made eye contact with her husband and was loosening her grasp of my arm. We walked slowly but with purpose through the crowd at the bar and zigzagged our way through the tables. Goran was the first to stand up and then everyone else in the restaurant, whether they knew us or not, followed suit. It was completely silent. I led her to the small and empty dance floor. Sasha had a silly smile on his face that I think he put there to keep himself from crying in front of everyone.

He whispered something into the ears of his new band mates and they started to play. It was love song from the old country that was unfamiliar to most of the younger people in the room, but very familiar to the older generation.

Rose whispered something in my ear that didn't register at first, but did the second time she repeated it to me through tears.

"This is our wedding song," is what she said in a barely audible tone as she watched Tomislav approach her. He got next to us and extended his good left hand to us. I respectfully passed Rose off to him and then stood next to them for a moment like a goofball, not quite knowing what to do next. Tomislav could tell that I was caught in a moment of confusion and offered some welcome advice, like he had over the many years we had been friends.

"Go get your own girl Niko," he said with a bright smile on his face as he and Rose started to slowly move around the tiny dance floor to Sasha's beautiful voice. I glanced over at our table and noticed a couple of the guys wiping what appeared to be something from their eyes. I would have guessed tears, but would have never called any of them out on it. Angela stood there in a trance as she watched her parents dance to a song they probably hadn't heard in many years. I made eye contact with my brother who was wiping tears from his eyes and even he adamantly nodded his head towards Angela.

I didn't want to upstage Tomislav and Rose, but I know that it's what they would have wanted. So I walked over to our table and took a look around at all the softies that had finally let their emotions get the best of them. I smiled and they all smiled through tear-glassed eyes back at me. I made my way over to Angela who was courageously trying to stifle tears.

Without words I extended my hand to her. She gently took it and we walked to the dance floor. When we got onto the dance floor, she immediately buried her head in my chest as we slowly moved to the beautiful music.

I rubbed Angela's back and held her tightly against me as she cried. I looked over and saw Tomislav and Rose in a tight embrace, barely moving, just letting the music sink into them. I took a glance around the room and realized that I couldn't have picked out a dry eye in the place even if I had been given a lot of money to do so. Then felt a tap on my shoulder and turned my head to see Tomislav.

"Do you mind if I have a dance with my daughter?" I didn't even say anything. I just pulled back away from Angela and gave her hand to her father's. I then took Rose's hand and started to dance with her. The entire crowd joined in a rousing ovation as the four of us made our way slowly around the dance floor. I tried to make eye contact with Angela as we moved, but she had her head buried in her father's chest and wasn't moving from there anytime soon. Rose took her hand off of my shoulder and planted it on my cheek.

"Thank you Niko." As I went to reply, a jolt of emotions shot through my body and into my lips, forcing them to quiver. I didn't want to cry at that moment, so I didn't say anything back. I just nodded, leaned way down and buried my head into Rose's shoulder as the crowd continued to cheer and applaud. Sasha wound down the last couple lines of the song. When he was done, he received he own rousing ovation that he bowed to not just once, twice or three times, but four times. I didn't blame him for sucking up all the attention that was being directed his way.

I had learned myself how empowering the feeling of being recognized for doing something special could be and I was glad that Sasha was experiencing his own dose of confidence rescuing adulation.

The four of us milled around on the dance floor for a moment and then I went to give back Rose to Tomislav. A surge of uninhibited ambition rocked my body as I took back Angela's hand. I smiled at Tomislav as he passed her back to me. He smiled at me and winked. As I held onto Angela's hand, I pulled on Tomislav's jacket sleeve and reeled him back to me. He gave me a look of surprise as I pulled him within whispering distance.

"I'd like to ask you for permission to marry your daughter." His eyes grew wide as he took a quick glance at Angela who looked convinced that our secret conversation was just more soccer talk. Tomislav looked for a minute like he was trying to talk, but nothing was coming out. His mouth moved, but silence prevailed. He then let go of Rose's hand and placed both his hands on my biceps, squeezing the air out of me on both sides. I noticed right away that his right hand was squeezing my shoulder just as hard as his left hand. Without making a scene, I stole a quick glimpse of his uncurled right hand holding tightly onto my shoulder. I couldn't see the details of his right palm because it was clasp tightly in my jacket sleeve. I was suddenly nervous and then scared that I had ruined the whole evening with one, possibly inappropriate sentence. But I was surprised to see that his right hand of all things, was clutching my shoulder so tightly.

"Yes," is all he said through squinted eyes and a tired, yet broad smile. He then gave me an affectionate slap on the cheek with the same right hand and snapped my head sideways.

Angela just stood there next to her mom, dumbfounded by all the affection that her dad and I were throwing around at each other in front of everyone. I don't even think it struck her or anyone else that he had opened that right hand of his.

I didn't want to make a big deal of it in front of everyone, because Tomislav wouldn't have cared for that kind of attention, but I did want to make a big deal out of my asking his daughter to marry me. So I jumped up on the little stage that barely fit the musicians and myself and confidently grabbed the microphone from a still-beaming Sasha.

I extended my hand to Angela for her to come join me up on stage. She relented at first by crossing her arms. I think she thought I was going to have her sing a song with me or something. But when I extended it again and pumped it for emphasis, she softened and jumped up with me. I could feel her clammy hand in mine as I raised the microphone to my mouth. Without turning her head to me she asked the same question everyone else in the room wanted to ask.

"What are you doing?"

"If I could have your attention everybody," I said. The room was almost completely quiet, except for an overzealous busboy that wouldn't stop clanging dishes in the back of the room as he hopefully bucked for his never-coming promotion to waiter.

"The MVP," shouted Goran from our table.

"You still got it old man," barked Mr. Nowinski.

"He got all that talent from me," yelled my brother. Even though we danced around the subject earlier in the alley, I don't think Angela really thought I meant what I meant. I felt compelled to make it all real while her dad was still here to see it.

"I just wanted to ask this very special person standing next to me a very important question."

The Gift of Stoppage Time

All the color in Angela's face suddenly escaped to other parts of her body as she raised her brow and fought with all her might to fight back an onslaught of tears. He looked down in front of me to see Tomislav and Rose standing side by side, holding hands. They were both smiling proudly and I knew that Tomislav had somehow leaked the news very quickly to his ever-loving wife of what was going to happen next. Angela was squeezing my hand so tightly that there was no doubt that the circulation had been cut off. It was something I was more than willing to live with, especially for this moment.

"Angela, will you marry me?"

I didn't have a ring or anything to give her. But I don't think she, nor anyone else in the room cared. She smiled and cried and then started nodding her head emphatically. I handed the microphone back to her Uncle as we embraced and kissed in front of everyone. The room erupted into raucous cheers again. I looked down to see Tomislav and Rose clapping enthusiastically for both of us. I then grabbed Angela's left hand with my right hand, faced the crowd and thrust our clasped hands into the air together, like referees did with prize fighter after a bout. Then Angela let go of my hand and jumped down to hug her mom and dad for what was probably the last time. I turned to Sasha who grabbed me in a spleen-shattering embrace while the cheering continued on around us. When I was done hugging him, the twins offered me congratulatory pats on the back. I was hoping to have Angela back, but when I looked down from the stage all I saw was her holding her mom and dad so tightly that even a crow bar wouldn't have done any good in trying to separate them. I knew it was a time for me to leave her alone with her family so I charged over to our table.

I was met with more hugs and pats on the head and back. A shot of Slivovitz appeared out of seemingly nowhere and I slammed it effortlessly. Sasha and the twins busted out into some modern cover tunes and a handful of couples hit the dance floor to strut what stuff they thought they had.

"I did not think that you were the marrying type," said my brother.

"I wasn't, until now."

"Congratulations," offered Mr. Nowinski as he handed me another shot of Slivovitz. I nodded thanks back to him as I reluctantly threw the burning shot toward the back of my throat. The Kid actually stood up from the table and gave me a hug.

"Yo man, you're not going to get all soft now are you, now that you're going to get married and all?"

"Don't ever use me and soft in the same sentence Kid," I said.

"You did good Niko," said Goran as he patted me with all his might on the back. It felt more like somebody was tickling me with a feather. Angela approached our table and grabbed Goran by the hand.

"What are you doing?" She turned to him only briefly to offer an explanation.

"We're dancing!" She led him quickly out to the packed dance floor.

"Come on guys, get out here," she demanded as her and Goran reached the edge of the dance floor. I think everyone knew that they would never hear the end of it if they didn't oblige her, so one by one, we all made our way out to the dance floor to stake our own little piece of real estate. Nobody could dance, except for Angela, but that was okay, because being afraid of anything was no longer in the cards for any of us.

The music played, we all danced and laughed and sang along with the words all out of tune. I looked around for Rose and Tomislav but couldn't find them. Then I glanced over at the bar and noticed them taking a shot together. I made eye contact with Angela and motioned over to the bar. Angela joined me at the edge of the dance floor, we clasped hands and we made our way over to her mom and dad. They had just finished a shot when we arrived. Rose grabbed me by the face and planted a big kiss on my cheek. Tomislav did the same to his daughter and then feigned like he was going to do it to me. We all shared a laugh.

"You two always belonged together," Rose said.

"I know," I said.

"Then what took you so long?"

"I had to make sure she would say yes," I said. Angela punched me.

"You had to give me the time of day," Angela said.

"What? I always had time for you."

"No arguing, no arguing, not now," pleaded Tomislav. Angela wrapped both of her arms around her parents and kissed them both on the cheeks. They did the same to her.

"We're just having fun dad. This has been the age-old argument with us...who didn't have time for who and why."

"Now it doesn't matter anymore, you both have time for each other," said Rose.

"That's right," said Angela.

"Absolutely," I said. I noticed Tomislav staring down at his right hand that was open wide. A long, wide scar ran from the base of his pinky to halfway up his thumb.

The Gift of Stoppage Time

"It's not so bad," he muttered to no one in particular.

"It's nothing," I said. He took his attention away from the scar and looked up at me slowly.

"It's never nothing Niko...it's always something," he said. He kept his gaze on me for seconds, emphasizing the point. I knew what he meant. Everything meant something, and I agreed with him now more than ever. Goran made his way over to the bar and grabbed Angela by the hand.

"You leave me all by myself and everyone now make fun of old man dancing by himself," he said faking a frown. Angela took his hand and made her way back to the dance floor with him. Rose, Tomislav and I all stood silently by the bar for a few minutes taking it all in. My legs and back were starting to ache pretty badly and I could feel myself running out of steam, but I wasn't about to shut it down before Tomislav did. I noticed Rose lean in to him and whisper something. He smiled and then laid a firm hand on the top of my shoulder.

"It's time for us to go," he said. I looked around the room at what had become an almost raging party.

"Now?"

"Yes Niko...now."

"Why? Aren't you having a good time?"

Tomislav looked over at Rose, who blushed slightly. "I'm having a great time Niko. But when the wife says it is time to go, you go. You understand, don't you?" I did understand, but didn't want him to leave. But then I caught myself being selfish, of only thinking about me and I knew that it wasn't what the night was about.

212

The Gift of Stoppage Time

It was about Tomislav and he wanted to leave with his wife and there was nothing wrong with it and nothing I could do anyway. I offered to walk them out.

"You want to say good-bye to everybody?" Right when I said it, I knew it didn't come out right. Tomislav knew that I didn't mean anything by it, but it sounded bad nonetheless.

"No, no, it's alright. We go." The three of us headed for the door. As we stepped out into the night, I noticed that the wind had stopped and everything was still.

"Let me go call a cab for you guys," I offered as I opened the door again to go back inside. Tomislav grabbed my jacket.

"We're okay Niko...we will walk." I looked at Rose who gave him a peculiar look, but then shrugged her shoulders like it would be no big deal.

"Are you going to be okay?" Tomislav let go of Rose's hand and came up close to me. He laid a hand on my cheek and patted it softly.

"I'll be okay Niko. You know that, right?"

"Yeah...I know," I said as I fought back tears.

"You don't need to worry about me Niko. I need you to worry about you...and my daughter, and Rose, of course." It was another thing about the old-school guys I admired greatly. They always cared for everyone else more than they cared for themselves.

"I know you'll be okay, but we're just getting started in there," I said as I wiped a tear that refused to be suppressed from my cheek.

"And I'm getting finished Niko," he said without a trace of regret in his voice. He confidently extended his right hand to me.

213

I clutched it tightly with my right hand and felt his strength pulse through my entire body. I didn't even feel the scar in his palm and we shook. He went back to Rose where he pecked her cheek and then wrapped her in his jacket to fight off the crisp night air. They turned from me and started making their way slowly down the block towards their house.

I watched them get to the corner and when they did, Tomislav paused and looked back at me. I could see him nod towards me. I returned the gesture and could have sworn he winked too. They turned the corner and disappeared from view. I just stood there motionless for minutes until the door of the restaurant flung open and smacked me across the back, knocking me to the ground. I looked up to see Cowboy Chris.

"You okay?"

"Yeah, if I can live with one kidney."

"Sorry pardner, but I thought that maybe ya were leaving with the old man." I was surprised that Cowboy Chris was naïve enough to think that I would have left my new fiancée back in the party to bail with her dad, but lots of strange stuff had happened tonight, so I cut him some slack.

"He just left with his wife," I said. Cowboy Chris fuddled in his pants pocket and then pulled out a watch. He held it in his hand and inspected it for a minute.

"Then this is for ya," he said. I didn't move, I just stared at the watch that Cowboy Chris held in his hand.

"What is it?"

"It's Tomislav's watch," he said. I knew what it was and who it belonged to, I was just in shock that it was being offered to me.

"Where'd you get it?"

"I used it to keep time for the game when the scoreboard clock broke...remember?" He kept extending it to me, but my hands refused to reach out for it.

"Why are you giving it to me?" Cowboy Chris could tell that I was freaking out a little bit, so he went and sat down on a bench that was in front of the restaurant.

"Tomislav wanted ya to have it."

"How do you know?" Cowboy Chris got up from the bench and came over to me. He wrapped his arm around me tightly.

"Because when I tried to give it back to him earlier tonight, he told me to keep it and give it to you after he left."

"That's what he said?"

"And he told me to tell ya to start counting up the time in your life instead of down. He said it's more fun that way." My hands started to shake as I reached out for the watch. Cowboy Chris waited for me to have a firm grasp of it before he let go.

"Thanks."

"Don't thank me, thank the old man pardner."

"Some day when I can...I will," I said as a huge gust of wind came up off the harbor out of nowhere. Cowboy Chris punched my shoulder and went inside to leave me alone. I inspected the watch in my hand. I flipped it over and read the inscription on the back of it just like I had in Tomislav's room earlier in the day. Instead of going back into the restaurant, I stood there in the cold for minutes, waiting for Tomislav to come back around the corner and to greet me with his wrinkled eyes and big smile again.

I wanted him to come back and ask me when the next game was going to be and when high school tryouts started and when Angela and I were going to actually get married and what the name of our first born child was going to be. I took a look down at the watch that I held in my shaking hand. I wiped the face of it off with my shirtsleeve and noticed that the little hand had stopped.

I looked back into the darkness where Tomislav had walked away from me just minutes ago with Rose and squinted, hoping to bring him back to me so that I could take him back into the party that celebrated his life. Unfortunately, I knew how it worked and I knew that it didn't work like that. So I put the watch on my wrist, slowly opened the door and went back into the party, just like Tomislav would have wanted me to do.

ABOUT THE AUTHOR

Mark Vincent Lincir grew up in San Pedro, California. He is the author of several books including A SOCCER LIFE IN SHORTS and THE WORLD NEEDS MORE BELLY RUBS. He writes at MarkVincentLincir.com and Soccer365.com.

15307898R00132

Made in the USA
Charleston, SC
28 October 2012